TRUE TO YOUR
CORE

Common Sense Values
for Living Life to Its Fullest

Jay C. Rifenbary

Author of the International Best-Seller *"No Excuse!"*

TRUE TO YOUR CORE
Common Sense Values for Living Life to Its Fullest

Published By Rifenbary Training & Development
Saratoga Springs, NY / jay@rifenbary.com
www.rifenbary.com

ISBN: 978-0-9832680-0-0
Copyright © 2011 by Jay C. Rifenbary

DEDICATION

To my wife Noni, whose love, internal strength, fortitude, and moral compass have taught me the meaning of commitment and strength of character.

To my children Nicole and Jared, who are the reflection of this journey. I will always cherish your empathy, patience, and belief in the goodness and heart of your father.

CONTENTS

ACKNOWLEDGEMENTS

Thank you to all those who share in the belief of a better self, a better family, and a better world. You have provided me the reason to wake up every morning, and you are the foundation for a sense of personal purpose in my life.

Thank you to Dawn Josephson for coming into my life at a professional crossroads. Your expertise and dedication to the art of writing has provided a renewed belief in just how far this message can travel and the positive difference it can make for so many.

Thank you to Summer Morris for her enthusiasm, professionalism, and creativity in fashioning a first-class and inviting cover design and logo.

INTRODUCTION

Do you know what you stand for—I mean what you really stand for—your core values? Most people do not. For a long time, I was included in that group of unknowing. Sure, I was always aware of certain values that were important to me or that I hoped I showed the world, just as you might be. But when it came right down to it, I did not know what was at my core.

Once I embraced the concept of core values, though, my life changed completely. Suddenly, I had a clear vision for my future and a way to get there. And the more I hold true to my core values every day, the better my life seems to be. The same can happen to you. This book will show you how.

If you've never given much thought to your core values, you're not alone. Most people don't devote much time, if any, to establishing core values for themselves. My first real experience with my own core values started on the basis of being accountable—of doing what I said I would do and not making excuses for any shortcomings. Over time, I realized that accountability is really just one piece of the puzzle, and that a person's core values are interrelated and run deep.

STRIVING FOR CLARITY

I freely admit that when I was a young professional, I had no idea what I wanted in life. I went from a career in the military to being a medical and pharmaceutical sales professional to being a business owner to being an author and speaker. It wasn't until my transition from business owner to my present day career that I realized knowing and staying true to my core values would set me free—free to be the person I knew I could be.

The journey of my life has also been one of self-discovery...and the journey is still going. My path of not knowing led me to what I wanted to discover. As it turns out, I'm not the only one who wants or needs this information. Since you teach best in life what you want to learn the most, it only makes sense that I share everything I've learned with you regarding core values so you can find clarity as well.

In this book, I present themes or areas of core values that deserve your focus and attention. The main areas addressed are Attitude, Accountability, Self-Respect, Personal Honesty, Life Balance, and Principled Leadership. Of course, you could have other core values; this book simply offers a way for you to discover which core values are important to you.

I chose these six focus areas for a reason. First, without the proper attitude, change of any kind is difficult. Your attitude in anything will either propel you forward or hold you back. With the proper attitude in place, you can begin to open your mind to the concept of core values. If you don't have any idea what you stand for and believe in—your core values—then it's difficult to be accountable and you're more likely to make excuses. If you're living a life like that, you can't have self-respect because you're not being personally honest and have no idea who you really are. As such, life balance becomes near impossible because you end up "drifting," following whatever idea happens to grab you at the time because you have no focus. Finally, because you lack focus and you're not behaving in a way that's reflective of what you stand for and believe in, you're less likely to be a principled leader and attain professional or personal success.

So as you can see, these six areas are interrelated. You can't focus on one without the other. And all the principles combined create a base of core values, which is the foundation of who you are.

You'll find that in order to grow and develop as an individual, a parent, a spouse, a business professional, a community leader, or anything in life you need a solid foundation. It's not just one principle or value that generates a degree of fulfillment, contentment, or success. To truly live your life to its fullest, you need a working relationship of all the principles in this book combined with any other core values you hold dear. Ultimately, understanding the relationship between these principles is really the foundation of developing the core values that reflect who you are.

WHY LISTEN TO ME?

That's certainly a valid question. After all, who am I to be telling you about core values? I'm not someone who is "all knowing." I'm not a famous football coach, astronaut, rock star, Olympic athlete, academy award winning actor, or high-profile CEO of a Fortune 100 company…and that's the point.

I'm not someone who is "special" or unapproachable. Quite the contrary, actually. I'm right there with you because I am just like you. I'm a parent, a spouse, and a business owner who has attempted to bring all the different facets of life into some type of collective understanding of how to conduct your life. Everything I share with you is a reflection of what I've encountered along the way. If I didn't overcome these challenges myself, I wouldn't know how to write about them or how to use my experiences to help others.

In fact, my message has resonated so well with the thousands of people who have attended my presentations and workshops simply because the insights are coming from a regular person. Sure, it's great to attend a seminar and listen to famous people, but what are you taking away from them? What learning points from their life can you really apply to your own? I may not be rich and famous, but the message in these pages is one that anyone can apply to their own life.

HOW TO USE THIS BOOK

Any kind of change you want to make in your life is a process. Meaningful change rarely occurs overnight. That's why I've broken these six core areas of development down into 52 strategies or common sense approaches. I know 52 is a big number—it represents the passing of an entire year. But is a year really that long? Look back at your own life. Do the years drag on endlessly, or do you often wonder where the years have gone? For most people, 52 weeks are gone in what feels like a blink of an eye.

While I hope it doesn't take you a full year to get through this book, I recognize the power of reflection. So while you may very well read these pages in just a few days, I would recommend you go back and choose one strategy per week to reflect on and develop in yourself. You will discover the more you reflect and reread these pages, the more the principles will become part of your thought process and life practice. By year's end, you'll be a more enriched and authentic person.

BE TRUE TO YOU

Now is the time to plan a path for yourself. Whether you already have some level of internal understanding of what your core values are, or if you've never given your core values a second thought, it's time that you formally solidify what your core values are and focus on them. You have the power to make major changes in your life and to live the life you want; knowing and living by your core values is the key.

This book will help you discover the power within yourself—the power to live your life to its fullest. Use the principles in this book to help guide your thinking and decision making from this day forward. Remember that the outcomes you experience in life are largely dependent on your choices and actions. Your actions, based on your core values, can create turning points in your life.

When you live a life consistent with your core values, you will clearly see the path that will lead you to happiness and fulfillment. You will have an attitude of success and will be fully accountable for any decision you make. As a result, you will live a life filled with self-respect and personal honesty because you are being true to yourself. When that occurs, attaining life balance and being a genuine principled leader will come naturally. Ultimately, when you live a life focused on your core values, you will be drawn toward your highest aspirations!

TRUE TO YOUR
CORE

Common Sense Values
for Living Life to Its Fullest

SECTION ONE

ATTITUDE
CORE

BE OPTIMISTIC – FOCUS ON YOUR ATTITUDE

"It is one's attitude at the beginning of a difficult
undertaking which, more than anything else,
will determine its successful outcome."
—William James

You can improve your life simply by changing your attitude. While that may sound simplistic, it's not simple for many people to do. Every day you can see examples of people who take a negative approach to life—from people who think and say negative and derogatory things to those who don't believe in themselves or their abilities.

Having the proper attitude helps you attain what you want in life. A positive attitude maintains focus on your goals and on the right path to achieving them. As a side benefit, your positive attitude can even inspire others to take action in their own lives.

When it comes to developing your core, a proper attitude is where it all starts. After all, you can have the best intentions to change your life, develop your core values, and attain your goals. But if you don't have the right attitude to propel you along the way, you'll likely have a difficult time on your path. That's why I'd like you to start our journey together by focusing on your attitude.

The principles in this section are designed to help you enhance your perspective on life. They're meant to help open your mind to new ways of thinking and looking at things. I want them to shake up your current thinking so you can let go of deeply rooted, long held beliefs that may be holding you back and diminishing your success. I also want the ideas presented here to lay the foundation for the rest of our journey together.

By keeping your attitude in check, you can create meaningful results in all areas of your life. Very soon, you'll be on your way to becoming happier, more successful, and more empowered to live by your core values every day.

1. BRINGING THE BEST INTO YOUR LIFE

Your attitude determines the overall course of your life. So I ask you, what do you attract into your life and why? Are the people and situations you attract positive or negative? Healthy or unhealthy? Respectful or abusive? Humble or egotistical? Selfless or self-centered? When was the last time you asked yourself such questions as, "Who are my circle of friends? Are they winners or whiners? Kind or critical? Giving or taking? Tomorrow or yesterday thinking? Thoughtful or thoughtless?"

Do you project to others your own vulnerabilities, and subsequently attract those who you think can fix those vulnerabilities? In reality, those who you believe can fix your vulnerabilities often possess similar or even more destructive vulnerabilities themselves.

Do you allow and enable a repetitive pattern of relationships and friendships that consistently result in the same disappointments? What kind of outlet do you gravitate toward to relinquish not having to be responsible for repairing yourself? Is that outlet one that invigorates you, or one that stagnates you? Does that outlet assist in breaking the pattern or reinforcing the same old pattern?

REFLECT ON YOUR ATTITUDE

I know these are many questions to ask you all at once. But I ask them for a reason. Through the course of my life's journey, I have found that reflecting and acting on these questions, especially during periods of personal doubt, has been extremely important and helpful. We all get caught up in the routine of life, but how often do you examine how healthy that routine may be? Are you hanging out with successful or oppressive people?

You likely know what the answers to the above questions should be, but what are your real answers—the answers that reflect your current reality and that subsequently determine your overall attitude?

People often ask me, "How do I break the patterns of behavior that reveal my weaknesses, vulnerabilities, and lack of self-respect?" The answer is to stop repeating the pattern. Granted, that's much easier said than done.

The first step is to acknowledge that a destructive pattern exists. Then, recognize the characteristics that initiate the pattern to be repeated. You can often gauge this by the status of your physical and emotional wellbeing. If a destructive pattern does exist, are you searching for a quick fix or working toward a durable repair to cope with those harmful behaviors?

YOU ARE THE COMPANY YOU KEEP

Regarding relationships, it is often easy to attach to a person who you believe possesses the characteristics you are lacking, because it directs you away from having to take responsibility for your own insecurities. It's also less stressful to repeat a relationship pattern that's familiar rather than construct a new pattern based on the personal core values you truly believe in. In reality, this person you are attaching to increases stress and creates more anxiety because the relationship provides erroneous justification to procrastinate working on your own internal dysfunctions.

Emotionally, you give yourself permission to forego dealing with your own issues by putting priority on the other person's issues. It's also common to use the other person's behaviors as an opportunity to validate your own value by enabling them, even if the behaviors are destructive in nature. You may become falsely dependent on the other person to "fix" you, or you may enable the other person's behavior to create a false sense of self-value. These behaviors tend to be ones you know, have experienced, or what you grew up with. Congratulations, and welcome to being codependent!

Codependents Anonymous defines codependence as "a tendency to behave in ways that negatively impact one's relationships and quality of life. This behavior may be characterized by denial, low self-esteem, compliance, and/or control patterns." Ouch! We are all codependent to varying degrees, and although these patterns can be deep rooted, whom we bring into our lives will either fuel the destructive symptoms or help dissipate them.

Therefore, it's imperative you make an effort to associate with emotionally healthy and optimistic people—people with a healthy attitude. Attract those in your life who are a positive force, not a debilitating one. Find those who you have common interests with, and together participate in events that reinforce the things and values you love.

FOCUS ON THE GOOD

Reflect on the things and experiences that have brought the most happiness to you. Those times where your joy and happiness were invalidated by others is not an excuse to live in misery, but an opportunity to reignite the passion for what inspires you to live. So celebrate the joys you cherish and attract those who mutually share those similar joys.

2. LESSONS IN ATTITUDE –
ARE YOU OPTIMISTICALLY CHALLENGED?

While in the Charlotte airport waiting on my flight to Albany, I noticed a young woman who was missing the bottom half of both her legs and was on prosthetic limbs. Surprisingly, she appeared to be quite comfortable and agile with them. Based on my background, my first thought was that she was in the military and was wounded while serving our country. I was tempted to approach her and ask the question, but I refrained, sensing it might make her feel uncomfortable.

After landing in Albany and arriving at the baggage claim, I again noticed this young woman. It appeared that her parents had met her, and they were welcoming her home. At this point, I could not help my desire to know. Moments later, I was introducing myself to her and her parents, and I asked my question.

She informed me that years ago she had been in a convoy south of Baghdad when an improvised explosive device (IED) exploded next to her vehicle, resulting in the partial loss of both her limbs. As I stood there listening, I was attentive to the fact of how gracious, positive, and comfortable she was sharing her story with me. In turn, I thanked her for her service to our nation and proceeded to give her a big hug. She responded, "You're welcome."

As I proceeded to exit the baggage claim I asked myself, "What did I wake up and whine about today? The weather? The world? My mistakes? What I don't have? Who did what to me years ago?"

Over the many years of experiencing humbling encounters such as this, I have learned to appreciate more and more the little blessings in life. I know that each day is a gift, that life is not what you are given but rather how you take it (attitude), and that friends and family should not be taken for granted.

A LESSON IN SELFLESSNESS

Another incident further reinforced my belief in the positive attitude that exists in our fellow human beings. After completing a full day training session, I was in a limousine being driven to the Orlando airport (provided by the generosity of my client). It was the peak of rush hour traffic. Approximately four miles from the airport terminal, the limousine broke down in the right hand lane of Semoran Boulevard, a very high volume thoroughfare in Orlando.

In a state of concern, the driver immediately made some calls on his cell phone in an attempt to get help. Unfortunately, his efforts were not working. We were stuck. Pondering the situation and knowing my flight was departing shortly, I realized I needed to take drastic measures. After learning there were no taxicabs in the area and that a replacement limousine wasn't available until after my scheduled flight departure, I made an Airborne/Ranger type decision and took matters into my own hands.

I exited the vehicle, grabbed my luggage, and attempted to flag down a potential "Good Samaritan" while screaming, "Is anyone going to the airport?" Since the broken down limousine had stalled traffic and caused a severe backup, initially all I heard were beeping horns and offensive language. However, within several minutes a young couple heard my plea, proceeded to stop their vehicle, and offered assistance. Seconds later, my bags were in their car, and I was on my way to the airport to catch my return flight to Albany.

After a brief introduction and some small talk, my new driver mentioned he needed fuel. We stopped at a gas station, and because of his kindness, I offered to pay for the fill up. Although he declined my offer, I insisted and shared with him that I felt it was the least I could do. Minutes after we departed the gas station, I was at the Southwest Terminal saying goodbye and thanking this couple who extended a gesture of kindness and went out of their way to assist someone in need.

CHOOSE YOUR ATTITUDE

These are just two examples of the kind of positive attitude I believe we should emulate. People who display a selfless attitude and graciousness continually remind me that kindness and generosity are still alive and well in the world. Remember: Attitude is a choice; make yours a positive one today and every day.

3. GO FOR THE GOAL – A SIMPLE APPROACH

Goal setting has been an established component in attempting to enhance one's personal and professional life, as well as a catalyst for human motivation. It has also provided guidance for organizational strategy and individual achievement. Unfortunately, the process of goal setting has become unnecessarily complex and over analyzed for individuals and organizations to utilize on a daily basis.

Allow me to simplify this individual process for you. Goal is defined as "the object of a person's ambition or effort; an aim or desired result."

So my first question to you is: "What does it mean to have a goal?" Second, "Do you have any goals in your life?"

To have a goal means you have direction for the path your future will take. To determine whether you have any direction for your life, here is a practical, undemanding, yet powerful question: When you woke up this morning, did you have something to look forward to?

If you did, then you have goals and direction. If you did not, then you need to reconsider what you're doing.

If you have more than one goal, which ones are most important? Rank your goals in order of importance. If you are able to execute that task successfully, then you have just established and prioritized your goals, and you are on a path of personal accomplishment.

KNOW YOUR PURPOSE

Having something to look forward to every day provides the energy to contribute positively to yourself and those around you, and helps to keep your attitude positive. It also validates that you as a human being matter, and that you have a purpose for existing. Without a sense of purpose, the excuse door opens, resulting in a loss of motivation, discouragement, frustration, and even depression. After all, how could you possibly be motivated if you have nothing you want to accomplish? Look at the number of individuals who emotionally and physically deteriorate when, in their own minds, they feel there is nothing to look forward to—they believe they no longer have purpose.

In her later years, my mother surrounded herself with people and daily tasks to maintain a personal sense that she still mattered. Whether it was her desire to play a round of golf, or take on the role of club historian, or continue to volunteer for the hospital, her daily activities provided her with a sense of value to herself and pride that she was still contributing to others and the community. By volunteering to causes she believed in and participating in activities she enjoyed, she lived life to its fullest. This continued desire to feel purposeful also stimulated for her fresh memories of happier times, people she has loved, and appreciation for the many blessings in her life.

The ability for all of us to feel we are contributing in some way to the world around us can make a substantial difference in our attitude and our daily emotional and physical well-being. Every day I personally make a point to recognize, acknowledge, and work toward the areas of my life that I look forward to. For example, these goals might include my next speaking engagement, workout, board meeting, lunch with friends, vacation, visiting my children, or searching for something new to experience to broaden my mind or challenge my body. There is so much life can offer if you have the confidence, sense of purpose, and proper attitude to take a chance on your future and discover your full potential.

CREATE YOUR FUTURE

Returning to those fundamental core values that reflect who you are will provide you the fortitude to manage those goals and provide you with an outlook on life that is optimistic and full of possibilities. Realize that having something to look forward to is essential to create yourself and your future. How you coordinate your efforts to accomplish those goals rests individually on you.

At this moment, my goal for you is that you wake up tomorrow morning with something to look forward to. Enjoy the day because you matter, have a purpose, and have the potential to positively impact those around you every day. Your attitude is the catalyst to begin that enjoyment.

4. OVERCOMING DISCRIMINATION
AND STEREOTYPES – HOW FAR HAVE WE NOT COME?

Discrimination and prejudice are sure signs of a negative or destructive attitude. Unfortunately, on a regular basis, I get a reminder of how far as a global community we have NOT come in overcoming our pre-judgment of others. Whether on television shows or in real life, I still see people dismissing a talented person just because of how the person looks.

Currently, people still cling to stereotypes and make assumptions about people's capabilities based on their appearance. The continual predominance of individuals judging the "book by its cover" validates the destructive social force that is alive and flourishing in all parts of the world. It seems that every day we witness a diversity of world hatred toward individuals, groups, religions, cultures, and nations. Will it ever stop?

Two questions every parent should discuss with their children are:

- As a society, have we reached a level of openness and non-judgment toward those around us that is equitable?

- How far have we come in regard to the stereotypes and prejudices we place on others based on appearance and general body language?

These questions should also be a continued recognition in your own life to lessen the stereotypical influences presented via many forms of media and technology.

CUT THROUGH FALSE ASSUMPTIONS

The fact is that we are continually challenged with deciphering through false misconceptions of what it takes and means to be successful. How many reality (or rather, non-reality) shows can you name that illustrate that point?

One definition of discrimination is "the ability to discern what is of high quality; good judgment or taste." How does someone achieve that, by appearance, race, creed, color, gender, sexual orientation, or age? I would hope we have made strides in regard to judging others by their character and not the color of their skin, as Martin Luther King, Jr. so poignantly shared in his "I Have a Dream" speech.

Stereotype is defined as "a widely held but fixed and oversimplified image or idea of a particular type of person or thing." It is quite apparent this continues to be a prevalent behavior by many on a daily basis. When we walk down the street and notice someone who may appear physically different, be from somewhere else, or may dress as though they are part of a different faith or culture, and then discern a conclusion of that person's character, how incredibly naïve and ignorant is that? And let's be honest…nearly everyone is guilty of this at some point. We all have preconceived notions of others based on the first physical impressions a person gives us, not necessarily on the person's character. It is diligent awareness of this deteriorating thought process that promotes a greater respect toward those we perceive as being different from ourselves.

THE FOUR E'S

One of the major themes within my seminar training sessions is the importance of treating others with dignity and respect. Over the years of growing as a person and challenging myself to further learn and understand life, I have discovered four areas that can assist all of us in decreasing our rapid judgment and stereotyping of others. I call them the four E's:

- Education
- Empathy
- Experience
- Equality

Educating ourselves about social and cultural history provides a foundation of understanding on a macro scale of people and their societies. I find it invigorating to learn about the advancements of civilizations and their contributions to world science, language, and economics to name a few. It generates an appreciation for where we come from.

Empathy, "the ability to understand and share the feelings of others," is essential to recognizing humility in ourselves and capabilities in others.

Experience validates education and fosters empathy. What is it like to walk in the shoes of those we stereotype or discriminate against? What does it feel like to have nothing materialistically, to be physically different, appear different, or feel out of place? Although some may never experience prejudice or discrimination, to participate in the lives of those who have heightens our own insight and appreciation for those who are the victims of directed unfairness.

Equality is being aware and accepting that we may have different talents, skills, and beliefs, but that we are all equally part of humanity.

Enjoy the benefits of being open-minded to the goodness of others on the inside, and understand that we are all part of a bigger world than ourselves. When you do, you'll elevate your attitude and gain an appreciation for life that is beneficial to all.

5. A LESSON IN GRACIOUSNESS

There have been many moments in my life where I have witnessed the warmth, graciousness, and hospitality of human beings. My experience in the Peoples Republic of China took that appreciation for those encounters to a new level.

I was invited to share my "No Excuse!" message with approximately 1,800 government and business officials in the city of Xuzhou, Jiangsu Province, a city of 9.5 million people, 375 miles south of Beijing. It was my first visit to China. As I was flying over the North Pole en-route to China, I felt both excitement and a degree of anxiousness.

Reflecting on the experience, words can barely express the overwhelming education I received from a human relations and personal awareness perspective. From the moment I arrived, the Chinese people treated me with a degree of dignity and respect I found both unexpected and humbling. The arrangements made, the sites seen, the people met, and the cultural insights gained were invigorating and fulfilling. My visits to the Great Wall, the Bird's Nest (Olympic Stadium), the Summer Palace, the Huai Hai Campaign Memorial Hall, the tomb of Gaozu (the first emperor of the Han Dynasty), the recently uncovered terracotta warrior relics, as well as lunches with the CPC General Secretary, Mayor of Xuzhou City, and the gifts exchanged, were just a few of the opportunities I was provided.

ATTITUDE IS UNIVERSAL

One event in particular added an element of human spirit to my trip that I was unprepared for. It was a dinner I shared with Wu Tianjun, VP and Chief Editor of Xuzhou Media. During our meal, he shared with me a story about his time in a communist re-education camp following the Chinese Revolution of 1949. He was a young boy at the time, and as I sat there listening, his comments were directed toward his belief in, and desire for, a better world.

I was sitting as a stranger, an American citizen, a believer in the democratic ideals of our nation, with an individual who was entrenched in the aftermath of a communist revolution and who was one of the top business figures in Xuzhou City. The enlightenment arrived when I realized we were not strangers at all. We had the same love for our community, our nation, our citizens, and our family, and a shared belief in the potential of humankind.

We as individuals from different parts of the world had much more in common than we did different. We were discussing life, success, and his genuine desire to learn from me how to implement ideas that would give his fellow citizens a belief in themselves, an understanding of the role of personal accountability, and a desire to eliminate the practice of making excuses.

The graciousness and humility he demonstrated toward me struck an emotional cord that I will forever remember and appreciate. I have always believed it is the dignity we demonstrate, the mutual respect we exchange, the attitude we take for ourselves and toward others, and an apolitical approach toward issues that will result in the betterment of lives around us. During that dinner, we gained an appreciation for one another, and a friendship.

ATTITUDE OPENS DOORS... AND CHANGES LIVES

I've always believed that things happen for a reason, and all souls who meet come together for a purpose. We attract what we project, regardless of whether it is a neighbor next door or a neighbor on the other side of the world. As a result of the graciousness I encountered during that trip, I gained an appreciation for the Chinese people, their culture, and their future.

Remember that no matter where you go, whether it is across town or across the world, you are always an unofficial ambassador for yourself, your family, your community, your company, or even your nation. Therefore, let us all make it a common practice to extend a positive attitude, graciousness, and hospitality to everyone we meet.

6. THE HYPOCRISY OF PROFESSED TOLERANCE

Why is it that many individuals who champion strong beliefs in tolerance are often the most intolerant when you disagree with them? Such people are especially dangerous to your development of a proper attitude, because they often appear to be a positive force in your life but then they give subtle or not-so-subtle messages to the contrary.

Tolerance is defined as "the ability or willingness to tolerate something, in particular the existence of opinions or behavior that one does not necessarily agree with." Why, then, is there such an enormous amount of fury between groups that disseminate varying viewpoints, personally attack individuals for a differing opinion, and yet promote themselves as ambassadors of tolerance?

As a proponent of liberty and freedom, I genuinely believe in the right for anyone to express and share their opinions and beliefs with anyone, anytime, at any place. However, righteous dismissal to opposing opinions by those who lobby for open-mindedness to their own agenda is mind-boggling and hypocritical.

For example, if I strongly believe in a woman's right to choose and I am a crusader for tolerance to that position and opinion, should not an opposing belief in a woman's desire for life be equally tolerated? If I am a proponent of gay marriage and that position is expressed respectfully, should not an expression of a belief in marriage between a man and a woman be uniformly regarded as well?

Anytime an opinion is defended with disrespect and distain toward the opposing position and person, it diminishes the credibility of the stance being defended. Next time you watch a news program, observe the proponents of the issues and the talking points presented, and then contemplate the elitism and derogatory behavior expressed by those who are challenged when they do not have the tact to respond to an opposing position.

ENCOURAGE TRUE OPEN-MINDEDNESS

All I'm asking is this: If you desire tolerance to a cause you believe in, then reciprocate with tolerance to those who are still attempting to understand your cause. Our professionalism (emotional patience) and humanity toward others should be a universal expectation, and those who genuinely express that humanity will have the credibility to add meaning and character to their positions.

When politicians turn their well-spoken statements of opinions into personal attacks directed toward their opponents, they diminish the enthusiasm of their constituency to support their causes. Negative campaigning should be a strategy of the past. It diminishes any character credibility the candidate may be attempting to solidify. Additionally, what does it say about society when we thrive on personal destruction of individuals? It demonstrates many would rather spend time on ridicule than contribute to the betterment of themselves and their community. This ubiquitous destructive attitude is promulgated throughout much of society as a way to distract us from our own responsibilities and accountability for our own actions.

An attribute of the human race should be the capability to be mutually respectful of others and display a professional tolerance for others and their differing viewpoints. There will never be a universal acceptance of every opposing opinion, but hopefully there will be a progressive understanding that insolent behavior and personal ridicule directed to those we disagree with does nothing to contribute in a positive way to the world around us.

TOOLS FOR TOLERANCE

Three behavior tools to assist in maintaining a level of professionalism needed to contend with disagreements are active listening, analytical evaluation, and amiable response.

- Active Listening is the ability to consciously listen to another's viewpoint without garnering an opposing position based on an emotional stimulus of the viewpoint being presented.

- Analytical Evaluation is the process of breaking down the facts of the position being taken to accurately formulate a credible response.

- Amiable Response is the ability to maintain a high standard of decorum and respond respectfully even in the midst of an emotional topic being addressed.

When practiced respectfully, tolerance provides civility within a diversely opinionated society. When tolerance becomes an excuse for abuse and ridicule of others, it destroys the fabric of mutual respect and social integrity. Let us all display a level of respectful tolerance while standing firm to the issues, beliefs, opinions, and core values we hold true.

7. FORGIVENESS CREATES FREEDOM

Have you ever met a person who likes to tell the story about what they should have done, might have done, or could have done? Or how about the person who shares the "if only" story—If only I had acquired a different job...If only I had been involved in a different relationship... If only I lived in a different community...If only I had a different degree...then I would be happy? Unfortunately, many people wake up every day using yesterday as an excuse to justify why they are miserable today. These people epitomize the characteristics of a negative attitude.

Realize that forgiveness is a powerful gift that releases us from the bondage of past failures, hurts, and disappointments. You cannot change yesterday, but you can make the choice whether to learn, grow, and move on from past mistakes and misfortunes, or allow them to control your emotional well being today and attitude in the future. The need for forgiveness in our lives is directly proportional to the degree of which we have failed, been hurt, or victimized. The more we experience these destructive encounters, a greater degree of forgiveness is needed to mend the damage done.

THREE LEVELS OF FORGIVENESS

Forgiveness of self is the first assignment for all of us. We have all failed at some point, but our failures teach us what we are capable of achieving. I believe a significant measure of a person is his or her ability to persevere through challenging times. It should be a goal for all of us to continue to look forward and not use past failures as present day excuses for being unhappy and unfulfilled.

Second, if you have ever attended a place of worship, you have likely heard the message about forgiving others who have hurt you. My question for you is, what does forgiving others have anything to do with others? The answer is absolutely nothing.

Whether the hurtful person accepts your forgiveness or not becomes his or her responsibility. Think about this for a moment. What are the people who have hurt you doing with their lives? Chances are they are moving on in a constructive or destructive way, but they are certainly not thinking of you. If they were thinking of you, wouldn't they want to mend the relationship, heal the hurts, and make amends from days gone by?

If we conclude they could care less about us, why would we allow them to emotionally live "rent free in our brain"? Evict them out of your head! You never forget the hurts, but if you do not forgive those who have hurt you, then you allow them to have control of your emotional well-being. Why would you allow someone else to control how you feel every day? That is your choice. It has nothing to do with those who have hurt you. The reason you forgive another person has nothing to do with the other person; it has everything to do with you. Let it go.

Forgiveness of environment is the third component to becoming free from the burden of baggage. It is a choice whether you allow the world, the weather, the war, the government, and the many other media driven disappointments to structure how you feel toward others and yourself. You cannot change many of the negative occurrences you witness and hear about every day, but you can change how you react to them. You can forgive the situation and not allow it to negatively impact your desire to be positive, optimistic, or continue to make a significant difference in the lives of others.

CREATE THE FOUNDATION OF YOUR ATTITUDE

Forgiveness generates the ultimate freedom—the freedom to enjoy life, to be less burdened, to embrace a positive outlook on life, and to be more joyous, giving, respectful, and selfless. So be free and enjoy the exhilaration of rescuing your emotional control from the grasps of the experiences and people who have taken it from you. Forgiveness will provide you a renewed outlook on life, a resurgence of positive energy, and a greater foundation of self-respect.

8. LIFE LESSONS – THE JOURNEY CONTINUES

During one of my corporate speaking engagements, I was scheduled to share two presentations with the managers and employees. Prior to the first seminar, the training coordinator asked if I would be willing to be interviewed by their communications team for an article in their newsletter. I appreciatively accepted the invitation.

The course of the interview was filled with many questions I am usually asked, such as: How did you proceed from West Point to inspirational speaking? How is the "No Excuse!" message being received? Who are your typical clients?

Upon getting close to the conclusion of the interview, the interviewer asked if she could ask one more question that was a bit more personal. I answered, "Of course." She then asked, "If your father were alive today, what would you tell him?" (My father passed away at the age of 49, when I was 11 years old.) You can imagine that the candidness of the question caught me by surprise. I was 52 years old when the question was asked, and in the 41 years since his passing, no one had ever asked me such a question.

As I contemplated for a moment, I sensed emotions that I had not felt in some time. Finally, I responded with, "I would not tell my father anything. I would ask him everything. What is it like to be a father, a husband, and a professional? How do you become those things? What are your values? What do you like to do? What are some of your philosophies about life? What inspires you to wake up every day?"

I would ask my father all the questions I never had an opportunity to ask him when I was a child. Upon further self-reflection, I realized that my desire for his presence, and the reality of his absence, prompted me to embark on a path to discover all the things I had always wanted to ask him. Thus, in the search to discover the answers I yearned for, I have been blessed to share that insight with others through my profession and my message.

LESSONS IN ATTITUDE

I learned a number of lessons from that simple question. Lesson number one is: "You teach best in life what you want to learn the most." I have always wanted to learn the things I had self-doubt about. As such, all the areas of life I had interest in and wanted to understand generated an excitement in me to share and teach that discovery and awareness with others. Ask yourself, "If you are passionate about something, isn't one of your greatest joys to share that something with others?"

For example, if you love to fish, ski, sew, study history, or have a hobby you enjoy, some of the most fulfilling times are when you share and teach that joy with others. Realize the interests in your life, the things you are passionate about, and the activities you enjoy the most will provide perspective of who you are, yield an understanding of the impact and influence others have had on you, and create a positive structure for your attitude. From a family perspective isn't interesting how we as parents pass down to our children many of the things we enjoy the most? Just examine friends and family acquaintances you have and how evident that historical pattern of interest repeats itself.

The second lesson is: "What happens to you happens for you." I certainly cannot go back those many years and change the passing of my father, but I understand that "life is not what you are given but how you take it." In my heart, I know I would not be the person I am, retain the family I have, nor have the opportunity to make a difference in the lives of others if that tragedy had not occurred. I cannot change the past, but only learn from the past, work with the present, and prepare for the future. I am sure there would have been many benefits in having a father figure and mentor in my life, but "it is what it is."

The final life lesson learned is to recognize that "we cannot use what we did not have in life to justify what we cannot be, cannot do, and cannot become." Doing so is simply an excuse for not taking accountability for your life and ownership for your actions. Therefore, enjoy what you love, learn from what you do, and help others along the way. These simple practices will elevate your attitude to new levels...and propel you to success and greater happiness.

SECTION TWO

BE ACCOUNTABLE – YOU HAVE NO EXCUSE!

"Life is not accountable to us.
We are accountable to life."
—Denis Waitley

Being accountable means taking responsibility for your thoughts, words, actions, and decisions. In fact, your accountability in life largely determines how you shape your future. Notice what I just said: "how you shape your future." Yes, you are ultimately responsible for your life's outcome, not other people, the economy, the government, your job, or any other outside force. You are responsible for your life, which is why you need to be accountable… starting right now (no excuse!).

For many people, taking accountability is difficult. After all, it's much easier to blame others, the past, the boss, the job, the parents, the world, etc. However, when you are accountable for everything in your life, you have the opportunity to build on your foundation of attitude so you can live your life to the fullest.

Additionally, as you increase your level of accountability, you will likely live life with a lighter heart. Knowing you have decided to no longer blame others or other things for your actions and results, you will feel stronger, less alone, and less frightened of the consequences. You'll be taking charge of your life and will feel empowered and free.

The principles in this section are designed to help you develop your level of accountability...to yourself, your family, your goals, and your life. They will help you persevere through times of doubt—times when excuse making and responsibility dodging are common—and they'll help you stay true to your core.

Ultimately, you'll realize that when you are fully accountable, you have power. You're no longer at the mercy of circumstances. You are the master of your destiny and have the ability to change your life. If a change needs to happen in your life, it's up to you to make it happen.

9. "WHATEVER" – DESTROYING ACCOUNTABILITY

Over the many years, the use of the word "whatever" has become a part of our daily conversation. Unknowing to many, "whatever" is having a very debilitating effect on our behaviors and resulting attitude toward personal and professional accountability.

To tolerate the use of "whatever" among our children only reinforces their lack of understanding about what it means to be accountable for their actions. Why did you lie? "Whatever." Why did you treat your friend with disrespect? "Whatever." And so on. It also substantiates for many children that it is appropriate to pass on blame and make excuses for failure and disappointment. It is essential that parents no longer tolerate the use of this word and that they set an example of not allowing "whatever" to be used concerning a decision being made or a behavior being disciplined.

In our organizations, leaders must recognize that the term "whatever" is having a significant impact on effective leadership and management. Frequent use of "whatever" in the workplace only undermines responsibility for failure and achievement, creates a lack of trust, and generates misunderstanding within the organization.

Additionally, it is extremely difficult for a leader to be effective when a "whatever" attitude exists among those being led. How can an organization be as efficient and profitable when its employees lack an understanding of the importance of taking accountability for their behaviors and performance? Can you imagine a board of directors of an organization who are in the midst of making an important decision responding to strategic and budgetary questions with "whatever"?

SET THE STAGE FOR ACCOUNTABILITY

Young people today are yearning for structure and discipline. They admire leaders who demonstrate strength of character and commitment to principles and core values. Peer pressure in our schools continues to be a formidable force in influencing the direction our children take with their lives. Compounding the problem is that you have adults who do not have any idea what they themselves stand for and believe in; they have no consistent core values of their own. So if I as a parent do not understand what I stand for and believe in, how could I possibly expect my children to have any idea what they should stand for and believe in? As a result, there are no parameters of behavior established. The children go to school and allow their friends to dictate how they should behave to artificially enhance their self-esteem.

It is my wish that parents, teachers, leaders, and anyone in a position of responsibility set an example not to tolerate the use of "whatever" at any time when an important decision must be made or when an individual must be held accountable for inappropriate behaviors or incorrect decisions. The establishment and reinforcement of personal and professional responsibility within our home and workplace, along with a consistent set of core values that guide our behaviors, provide the foundation for a strong and disciplined family unit and for a productive and profitable workforce.

10. BLAME STORMING SESSION

Those who live in the southern United States are familiar with hurricanes. However, there is another hurricane brewing that will hit the entire country, if not the world. This hurricane is named Hurricane Blame. I am not sure if it is a category 5 yet, but it appears to be gaining strength as each day goes by, and the destruction could be devastating. As "Blame" becomes stronger, and the role of personal accountability becomes less and less of a barometer in evaluating the health of our society, the need for social values and principles deteriorate into irrelevancy. Eventually, our society has the potential to capsize.

We have already seen the destructive nature of "Blame" in our schools, corporations, government, and more. Why do we need honesty and integrity when it is someone else's fault for our failings? We don't! "It was my dysfunctional family." "I did not have an adequate role model growing up." "There are reasons I had to lie." Really?

TAKE BACK CONTROL

Why are manners and respectful behavior necessary when it is the fault of the Internet, television, and peer pressure for a child's misbehavior and not the child themselves? Why do we need to be fiscally responsible with our own finances when we can fault the government for being irresponsible with the nation's finances? Why do we need to be professionally responsible for our work performance when it is my manager's fault for not listening to me? Why do we need to be personally responsible in our daily lives when it is the fault of society and the media for sensationalizing irresponsible behavior? The way the winds of thought are blowing presently, if I falter, there must be something or someone I can blame. Excuses are the hidden undercurrents that fuel the storm.

Every time we blame, whine, and/or complain what do we give up? We relinquish control and give it to some other entity. How could you possibly be content and fulfilled when you believe it is up to someone or something else to be responsible for your life?

"Wait just a minute," you may be thinking. "Isn't it someone else's responsibility—my place of work, the government, my place of worship, my community, society—to make me happy and fulfilled?" Granted, they all may play a role, but the reality for you and me, from the moment we wake up in the morning to the time we put our heads on that pillow at night, is that our choices and our decisions structure what we become and eventually determine how happy we are. It is the personal example we set every day by our actions, and taking personal responsibility for those actions, that determine how easily we get caught in the hurricane's path. Once again, those choices and decisions stem from an understanding of what we stand for and believe (i.e. our core values). The consequences from just whining about hurricane "Blame" and not taking the actions to prepare for and minimize its impact will be disastrous.

I encourage you to no longer put up with the whiners, blamers, and excuse makers. Rather, hold strong to becoming "No Excuse!" people and understand that you set an example of personal accountability to yourself, your children and those you influence every day. Do not let hurricane "Blame" get the best of you.

11. CORE VALUES FOR HOMEWORK

One of my major themes within my training program is the establishment and implementation of a set of core values within an organization. These core values should reflect the leadership's fundamental approach toward how business is conducted and how clients view the organization. Core values provide the parameters of behavior to hold ourselves and others accountable, and they offer a more complete evaluation of performance and decisions being made. It is also imperative that these core values be defined for the employees and the entire gamut of the workforce.

It's human nature to define the words we hear, not only by what the dictionary may state, but also based on our life experience with that word. That's why I can say the word "integrity" and everyone may have a variation of what the word means based on their life experience with it. I often have younger people in my workshop sessions. When I ask them, "What does the word 'integrity' mean?" they often reply, "I have no idea." This is why it's important that you define what you mean by what you say.

During the course of my travels and training, I have encountered organizations with a firm set of core values that are reflective in the leadership and the employee base. However, it is extremely important for the leadership to constantly review, remind the entire team, and consistently define what those values are and will continue to be. The resulting benefit is enhanced trust and accountability. This leads to better communication, which extends to better efficiency, productivity, and eventually greater profitability.

ACCOUNTABILITY IN THE BUSINESS OF LIFE

Here is the "homework" twist to all this. I also conduct training sessions for small groups of CEOs and senior leadership across the country. In the course of discussing core values, I always enjoy seeing the visual response of senior leadership when I ask them, "Have you ever sat down at the dinner table and asked your children and family, 'What do you think the core values of our family might be?'"

There is always a brief hesitation and pondering that occurs when I ask that question. So, we can establish core values for our organization, but most people do not take the time to establish core values for their family? We often assume the children know, but in reality, the assumption is incomplete. It must be brought to the surface. You need to discuss your family's values to solidify a foundation of understanding. Of course, this does not only apply to senior leadership, but everyone reading this.

The wonderment of this "core value" homework assignment is when a child says, "Honesty should be one of our core values," the child has to then take ownership for what she just said, which allows you as a parent to hold her...what? "Accountable" It works!

We established four core values in our family, and they are as follows:

- Always be honest
- Always do the best you can
- Treat people with respect
- When you start something you do not quit midstream

Would my children sometimes fight these values growing up? Absolutely. But now that they are grown I have noticed that these core values have provided a basis for their sense of self-respect and confidence, their ability to tackle the difficulties of life, and their having to make decisions they must take ownership for.

Take the time tonight to sit down with your family and ask them, "What are the core values of our family?" It will pay huge parenting dividends down the road, because it will provide those parameters of behavior and a structure to build your children's sense of accountability and self-respect.

12. PERSONAL INITIATIVE – DEFEATING PROCRASTINATION

When conducting my seminars, I often ask leaders, "What social trends are you witnessing that are challenging your ability to effectively lead others?" A common response is, "An acceptance of mediocrity and the lack of initiative among employees."

The existence of this social trend decreases accountability, promotes procrastination, and is devastating to the efficiency, productivity, and profitability of an organization. It depletes individual creativity, innovation, and a spirit of risk taking because of the lack of assertiveness prevalent in the workforce.

This same attitude, when transferred into our personal lives, has similar consequences. Initiative is defined as "the ability to assess and initiate things independently, the power or opportunity to act or take charge before others do, an act or strategy intended to resolve a difficulty or improve a situation, a fresh approach to something." Assertive is defined as "having or showing a confident and forceful personality."

Do you personally accept mediocrity, lack initiative, and procrastinate in regard to your potential to excel in life? Or, are you taking the steps necessary to become increasingly assertive in making decisions, accomplishing tasks, and welcoming opportunities to expand into a better you?

RELY ON YOUR CORE VALUES TO STAY ACCOUNTABLE

Personal initiative plus assertiveness eliminates procrastination. A lack of assertiveness and initiative stimulates the fundamental reasons behind procrastination. Those are the fears of failure and the unknown. Without having a confident personality and the belief in yourself to act independently, putting off what you know needs to be done is easy and sustains those fears. In addition, deciding a task is too difficult or stressful to initiate and complete is only an excuse for not taking ownership for the responsibilities you have created in your personal and professional life.

It is the understanding and implementation of your core values that provide the strength to be assertive and take the initiative. Your core values provide a foundation to execute present and future actions. Structured and defined core values in an organization create the blueprint to hold employees accountable as they enable us to hold ourselves accountable.

Procrastination diminishes self-esteem because it delays acting on the core values that enhance personal pride and self-respect. If you do not act on what needs to be done, how can you grow as a person and as a professional?

Procrastination can be aligned conceptually to a lack of forgiveness because both behaviors allow for incompletes and unresolved issues. Both human frailties direct energy toward a path that is self-destructive. The burden to carry what still needs to be completed drains the human spirit and stifles initiative. All of us know individuals who cannot let things go, whether it be hurts from past relationships, employment, or even personal failures. Are you one of those individuals? Procrastinating on not forgiving yourself or others only creates further frustration, anger, and disappointment because it directs wasteful energy toward what was, instead of directing productive energy toward what can be.

What do you have to lose by being assertive and taking the initiative? If you are honest in your attempt at resolving an issue or accomplishing a task there is nothing to lose. You can only gain from the success or learn from the mistakes made in the process. As many notable leaders have said, "It is better to have tried and failed than to have never tried at all."

COMMIT TO BANISHING PROCRASTINATION

Five basic practices to overcome procrastination are:

- Believe in yourself that the task at hand can be accomplished successfully

- Set aside time and energy to initiate what needs to be completed

- Manage effectively and follow through with the process to its completion

- Evaluate the completed task by thoroughly reviewing the process to assess ways to improve in the future

- Celebrate the achievement by appreciating yourself and recognizing those who have assisted in the achievement.

Anyone can make a decision not to do something. But if that something is important and contributes to the betterment of you, your family, and your profession, then step up to the plate. Take action and hit the home run by thinking more of others than yourself. Initiative combined with assertiveness creates a team destined to succeed, and you are that team.

13. PERSEVERANCE – AN ACCOUNTABLE CHOICE IN DIFFICULT TIMES

Perseverance is defined as "steadfastness in doing something despite difficulty or delay in achieving success." Has there ever been a time in your life when you just wanted to give up on an endeavor you initiated? A moment when you wanted to give up on your dreams because the path to get there appeared too daunting?

At some point, everyone has had to make the decision of whether to persevere through a circumstance, situation, or challenge. I certainly have experienced those times, and I possess the emotional benefits and bruises from past attempted ventures as a result. Two major reflections for me that immediately come to mind were the decisions to persevere through West Point and the U.S. Army's Ranger School. Even more significant was the decision to continue to pursue a career in public speaking and consulting after several major setbacks.

RISK VERSUS DESIRE

The choice not to quit did prove to be beneficial in the long run, but not without sacrifices along the way. Through experiencing the successes and failures of many such journeys, I have concluded the primary factor in deciding to persevere or not is a result of the competition between desire and risk. If desire for your life's passion outweighs the risk in attempting to achieve that passion and you quit, there is a strong likelihood that you will regret that decision now and/or in the future. However, if it is determined the risks outweigh the desire, it may become apparent to change course from that desire or dream.

When we're younger, the risks may be minimal because we have fewer responsibilities to contend with and less to lose in "going for it." For example, if I do not have the responsibility of family or an established career, then the risks to my relationships and financial security would be nominal. On the other hand, the more responsibility you create in your life journey, the more difficult it is to have the freedom to pursue a different dream or a new career.

Many of us reach a point in life where we are inspired to invigorate our future—we want to create challenges and potential new careers. Does mid-life crisis ring a bell for anyone? Personally, I came very close to destroying the things I had created to pursue a goal I was unsure I could succeed at. I am thankful and humbled for the belief my wife and children had in me to see my desire come to fruition. As a result, their support in the process of the attainment of that goal made the risks less prominent.

ACCEPT RATHER THAN EXPECT

If you decide the risks outweigh the desire, you need to take the necessary step to alleviate the emotional struggle and disappointment you may experience by not pursuing that desire. That step is to comprehend the importance of becoming more accepting than expecting. You may desire more in your life, but if the risks to achieve that, such as destroying your family, your health, and your finances might occur in the process, it might be necessary to forgo that goal. Therefore, become more accepting of the choices you have made and the life you have created.

Another advantage to acceptance versus expectation is to realize that if you are never satisfied and always expecting, how can you be content and at peace with yourself? I am not suggesting you give up on your aspirations, but rather that you fully understand the potential sacrifices needed to be made to achieve that goal.

A final advantage of accepting rather than expecting is the reduction of stress in your life. Many of us are high expectation people. I realized later in life that I would get myself in the most trouble when I would put all my expectations on everyone else. Well, not everyone is like me, and not everyone is like you. When I accepted this understanding, my stress declined and I was happier day to day. It was a relief not to expect the world and everyone in it to be on my agenda. This does not mean I am accepting of behaviors that violate my values, or of performance that is less than expected. But what I have come to realize is the total benefit of understanding what makes others wonderful.

Enjoy new peace in your life when you reflect and appreciate what you have already created and accomplished.

14. GLOOMY? SNAP OUT OF IT!

At the United States Military Academy at West Point, we had a phrase that we used for the winter months of the year: "Gloom Period." Gray buildings, gray skies, gray uniforms, gray skin complexions, and gray weather all contributed to a feeling of depression and a yearning for sunshine.

Many people confront this period of "blah," whether during the winter months or any time of year when a struggle occurs. Some people succumb to the gloom and the self-doubt that blankets their normal cheery outlook on life. Even I find it difficult at times not to fall into this precipice of reflecting on my life's journey in an other-than-healthy and optimistic appraisal.

By its nature, "gloom period" fuels the senses to be less positive and less energetic about the present and even the future. There are also times where you may feel trapped inside your own little cocoon of thought because a situation makes events appear unbearable. You may even find yourself doubting your abilities in progressing and creating the life you want. However, when you doubt yourself, there is usually a bigger issue to be addressed. We all experience self-doubt at times, but when it raises its ugly head and begins to stifle your day-to-day enjoyment, it is time to take action.

"Gloom period" adds another excuse to justify being miserable. My recommendation is to snap out of it and take accountability for your attitude and behavior!

TAKE CHARGE OF THE GLOOM

When you're feeling gloomy, it's time for the rubber to meet the road—for you to show your true personal confidence, attitude, and outlook on life. It is where a reflection of core values and what you stand for and believe in is extremely beneficial.

In regard to business, do you sit around and whine about the economy, or do you take the "bull by the horns" and take the initiative to be more creative, innovative, and ingenious? In regard to your personal life, do you reflect on what should have, could have, and would have been, or do you recognize yesterday is gone and you cannot use it as an excuse for not working toward being happy and fulfilled? Questioning where you were, where you are, and where you want to be is healthy, but only if the outcome of that reflection is recognition of learning from the past, acting on today, and planning for the future.

Hypothetically, I could sit and mope about business being slow, conferences being cancelled, and companies not spending money on speakers, or I could reevaluate and take the action necessary to reinvent my business and persevere. It is harder to leave your comfort zone and attempt a new approach toward the future than it is to generate the excuse that outside forces are wrecking your life.

YOUR ACCOUNTABILITY ACTION PLAN

Do you "couch potato" and paddle in a pool of self-pity, or do you take the steps necessary to energize your mind, body, and spirit? Do you blame others, or do you take accountability for the doubts you may have and take action to overcome those insecurities?

Seven steps for overcoming gloom are:

- Call a friend and go out for a bite to eat; get out of the house

- Turn off the news and read or watch something uplifting

- Be with positive and energetic people

- Volunteer in something that will help others and take your mind off of gloom

- Eat healthier, exercise more, and celebrate the gloom (have a gloom party!); it's temporary

- Project optimism by a smile, gesture, or a kind word

- Reenergize the core values you believe in

Take responsibility for your thoughts, feelings, and actions. Work through the gloom, because sunny skies are always around the corner.

15. OUR SPOILING SOCIETY – A DETRIMENT TO HEALTHY CHARACTER

What happens when we *spoil* a child—when we give them things they have not earned? Two definitions for spoil are "diminish or destroy the value or quality," and "harm the character of (a child) by being too lenient or indulgent."

Generationally, it has been well known that spoiling a child does little to enhance their sense of accountability and self-respect. It also breeds a sense of entitlement, which has become rampant in many aspects of our society. A sense of entitlement diminishes a person's desire to put forth effort to achieve, because effort is not needed if someone is already expecting what they have not earned.

Do you genuinely believe you are owed, and if so, by whom? When you are given something you did not earn, the value of what is given becomes much less significant in your mind. When we as individuals do not act upon the values that frame who we are, our own sense of self-respect is detrimentally impacted as well. Why would we take pride in something we have not earned? Why would we take pride in ourselves if we have not earned who we are?

Each day is an opportunity to build upon who we are by acting on the values that form the foundation of our character. Why, then, do we continue to overindulge our youth with stuff, and many in our workforce with false expectations of what they deserve or have earned? Both answers revolve around the ease to which we satisfy the demands of others.

INSTILL ACCOUNTABILITY IN OTHERS

In regard to our children, it is much easier to bow down to the "everyone else is doing it" or "everyone else has one" acceptance attitude than it is to take the time and effort to instill in our children the value of earning what they want and being accountable for their actions. The lessons taught to our children by "working in the trenches" build discipline, character, and self-respect. The largest benefit to a child is the understanding that their efforts will create the life they want—one filled with personal responsibility.

In regard to workers, it is much easier to maintain control and power over a workforce by promising benefits and pay increases without accountability and performance standards than it is to reward based on measured accomplishment and improvement. Look around to see the negative impact that entitlement patterned industries have had on quality of performance, value of product, education of our children, fiscal responsibility, motivated employees, and industry sustainability.

When the bar for any defined achievement is lowered in any area of expected performance, the value and credibility of the achievement is degraded. An example of this would be lowering performance standards to accommodate lower performing individuals. What message does that send our children? Do not work as hard because the system will adapt to you?

Here are two steps for assisting anyone in his or her understanding of the value of effort:

- Have them feel the sense of accomplishment by achieving a task based on their effort alone

- Instill in them an understanding that personal effort builds strong character, increases self-respect, and reinforces the values they espouse too.

People are much happier and fulfilled in life when they have generated a sense of purpose and accomplishment on their own. Seize The Day!

16. STOP THE SELF-SABOTAGE – YOU ARE VALUED

How do you handle disappointment, regret, stress, frustration, sadness, risk, or just life in general? What do you do to escape? Is there a repetitive reaction or behavior you participate in when you encounter life's ups and downs? Is the response you take healthy or unhealthy? Have you ever said to yourself, "I need a beer…a cigarette…a piece of chocolate or two (or some other addictive substance) to handle this situation?" Even the behaviors we perceive as being healthy can be substitutes for emotional accountability: "I need to exercise again…run further…work longer… volunteer more…lose more weight…study more…etc."

I can recall many instances where I would utilize an outside perceived comforter to soften the struggle of life, the outcome of an event, or the stress of a relationship. I am tested each day with my ability to contain patterns of behavior that I know to be self-destructive.

How often do you take the time to think before you act? How often do you participate in behaviors and not reflect on the possible cause or outcome of that behavior? Of course, I am referring to irrational excess and consistent patterns of actions, although many sabotaging behaviors in moderation can be incredibly debilitating as well, such as substance abuse. Years may pass and you may ask yourself, "How did I ever go down this road of personal emotional and physical deterioration?" The result of such behaviors may not be a totally sabotaged life, but the day-to-day internal battles that stimulate those behaviors contribute to emotional and physiological struggles that are extremely debilitating.

YOU DESERVE SUCCESS

We all have had countless experiences as children that we can examine to aid us in understanding why we are the way we are, but then what? The deep-rooted understandings of these dysfunctions can be left to the therapist to decipher. All I am asking is that you use common sense in recognizing what you may be doing to yourself in the course of handling life.

I want you to be happy with yourself. It is always easier to make the excuse than it is to assess where you are with yourself and incorporate the core values you believe in, act on them, and build a greater sense of personal accountability and self-respect. The key question to ask yourself is, "How are my behaviors impacting those around me, especially my loved ones?" Most individuals know when they are being harmful to themselves, which then translates into the task of taking personal accountability. However, how often do you reflect on how your behaviors may impact those around you, and do you take accountability for that?

As our society continues a growing pattern of self-rationalized excuses for misbehavior, an "all about me" demeanor, and entitlement attitude, having belief in self-determination becomes more challenging. Stop the self-sabotage and begin to develop the person you want to be and believe you can be. Understand that there are people who love you, believe in you, count on you, and need you. If you impact another person, you have a responsibility to that person, and personal accountability is key.

DEAL WITH IT...NOW

Are you taking ownership for your life, dealing with the occasional or constant unhappiness, or are you continuing a pattern of behavior to shelter yourself from feeling what you do not want to feel? If you berate those around you when you are under stress, what are you protecting? Where are you vulnerable? If your opinion must always matter, why? If you need to self-medicate to where you cannot feel, what are you not dealing with?

It is not fair to you and especially those around you to be miserable and create misery. We all doubt ourselves, including me, but how extensive are those doubts and how are they impacting others? The first major hurdle in overcoming any self-sabotaging behavior is to acknowledge you are doing it and take accountability for your actions or inaction. The next step is to listen to those around you who are the recipients of those self-destructive behaviors.

It will always be humility and acceptance of your vulnerabilities that will be the breakthrough in persevering through what you dislike about yourself. Remember, you can only love others to the extent you love yourself.

17. ENTITLEMENT – A CATALYST FOR CATASTROPHE

There is a growing trend toward a societal sense of entitlement progressing across this country, and it is only becoming stronger and more evident as political and business leaders market themselves as the caretakers for all of our nations' citizens and non-citizens' problems and disappointments. It is not the responsibility of some other entity to take care of our personal problems and correct our own mistakes. It is the responsibility of each individual to learn from mistakes, take the necessary steps to persevere through their own personal challenges, and be accountable from that point on for their life choices.

I do not believe we are entitled to things we have not participated in or made an attempt to earn. When an individual, and subsequently a society, begins to become dependent on someone or something else to take care of them, individual creativity, innovation, entrepreneurial spirit, and personal accountability deteriorate rapidly. Why take the steps to excel in any endeavor when there is no incentive or reward for putting greater effort into the endeavor than someone else?

This entitlement attitude also has a significant impact on an individual's self-respect. If you did not know how to earn what you have, or do not know how to earn what you want, how could you have any degree of self-worth? When we spoil our children by giving them things they have not earned, the destructive aftermath of a lack of self-worth and a lack of accountability becomes evident.

LEAD BY EXAMPLE

What message do we send our children when they are inundated with propagandized rational that they should have the same as everyone else without having to earn it? They learn that life's successes and failures are a result of someone else's actions—the absolute opposite of accountability. Another result is that mediocrity becomes the norm, and apathy toward achievement is accepted. The ability and right to choose the course of your own life will be over, and the principle of self-determination will be lost forever.

Your core values should not include the idea that your life is not yours, nor is it the instrument of some other entity that controls it. Your core values should include principles that encourage personal ownership for your behaviors, and an attitude promoting the ability to structure your own future—the two key factors of accountability.

As a society, we have a responsibility to help our fellow citizens in need. To make sure a child does not starve, a victim of poverty does not suffer, and that care and aid are provided to those who have truly been victimized or who have been on the receiving end of nature's wrath. As individuals, we have a responsibility to ourselves to ensure we take ownership for who we are and the decisions we make. What can we do as parents and citizens?

- Do not set an example that it is someone else's fault for the mistakes we make and have made.

- Do exemplify behaviors that encourage self-reliance, initiative, accountability, creativity, integrity, and other core values that enhance an understanding of personal life ownership.

ACCOUNTABILITY UNLOCKS YOUR POTENTIAL

We all have the ability to become aware of our potential as individuals and to build and act upon the unique skills and talents we possess to expand a greater understanding of life and make a positive impact on one another. A world where everyone is patterned to be the same and controlled by the few will only diminish our ability to reach our full human potential.

Take the time to assess your own future—the current decisions that have to be made and the path upon which those decisions are implemented. With a solid foundation of core values, an understanding of self-reliance, an acceptance of personal accountability, and an attitude of selfless behavior, how could you not be happy? Relying on something else to manage your life is analogous to being behind bars. You are trapped from creating the future you want. Enjoy the freedom that comes with accountability because you will have earned it.

SECTION THREE

BE RESPECTFUL – YOU OWE IT TO YOURSELF

"Respect yourself and others will respect you."
–Confucius

How can you achieve success in anything in life if you don't first respect yourself? Why would you even want to? You'll always doubt what you can achieve if you don't respect yourself.

When you have a positive attitude and take accountability for yourself, you'll feel better about who you are—you'll respect yourself more. When that occurs, your success is eminent because your level of self-respect affects all your thoughts and actions.

The fact is that how you feel about yourself determines the direction you take and the decisions you make. How and what you think about yourself determines what you become. Your level of self-respect structures what you achieve.

Unfortunately, society today sometimes makes self-respect difficult. We are bombarded with so many messages about what determines our worth in life. For example, commercials tell us that people will only like us for the things we eat, drink, and own. Television shows promote the idea that other people have a better life or more value. News programs continually remind us that someone (sometimes us) is to blame for all of society's woes. With so much negativity coming at us, it's no wonder that many people have little to no self-respect.

The principles in this section are designed to help you bolster your level of self-respect. My goal is that you learn to trust yourself, your talents, your special attributes, and your inherent gifts so you realize that you are a valuable and worthwhile person. Only when you see and value your own importance can others value you.

When you respect yourself, others take notice. You become a role model for success and attract like-minded people into your life. That's when great things really start to happen because you have the synergy of many working together for a common result. But people will only follow and want to be with you if they sense you respect yourself…and respect them.

Know yourself and respect yourself, and then watch your future change for the better.

18. SELF-ESTEEM – THE GIFT MYTH

During the course of defining, explaining, and discussing self-esteem and self-respect in my training sessions, I actually apologize to my younger audience in regard to this important principle of success. Why? Over many years, Baby Boomers (which I am a part of) have created a generation of young people who, in many cases, believe it is more important to feel good than do good.

When my two children were attending elementary school, I can vividly recall when the new fad for improving education was to provide students with a greater sense of self-esteem. How do you accomplish that? Tell them how wonderful they are? I can assure you that enhancing self-esteem is not putting a purple star on a five-year-old student's forehead and saying, "Feel good about yourself." That may be a tool for encouragement, but it does not instill self-esteem and it certainly doesn't lead to self-respect.

"Self-esteem" is defined as "pride in oneself." Upon further page turning in the dictionary, "pride" is defined as "a sense of one's own dignity or value; self-respect."

How does someone attain a sense of dignity, value, and self-respect in their life? Does some spiritual entity come down from the sky and pronounce you a person of self-respect? I think not. A common excuse I often hear people say to justify relinquishing their personal responsibility is, "I have low self-esteem." In a professional and empathetic way, my usual response is, "What are you doing about it?"

VALUE YOURSELF

A sense of dignity, value, and self-respect / pride in oneself / self-esteem is not given to a child or an adult; it is earned. How do you earn it? Through your day-to-day behaviors. As such, your behaviors should be based on your understanding, or at least an awareness, of what your core values are.

Core values are established, or not established, in a child by their parents or the family structure they are raised in. Without core values, there is no basis for personal accountability, and without personal accountability there is little self-respect generated. This illustrates how core values, accountability, and self-respect are interdependent of one another. It also provides the evidence needed to understand the relationship between a person's level of self-esteem and the impact of peer pressure. Without an understating of what I stand for and believe in (my core values), I am less likely to hold myself accountable, more likely to be indecisive when my sense of self is challenged, be drawn to what others think I should do, and as a result, behave in a way that does not reinforce a sense of pride, dignity, or self-respect.

A key indicator of an individual's level of self-esteem is their ability or inability to make decisions. Two major fears all human beings have are the fear of failure and the fear of rejection. Fear of failure is fear of self, and fear of rejection is fear of others. These fears stem from how we were parented. Personally and in the workplace, if the fears of failure and rejection are so strong that it prevents an individual from being decisive, it can be a reflection of their lack of self-esteem. Why? Because the individual does not have the inner strength to stand up for their convictions and beliefs, because they do not know what their core values are, as a result they doubt their own value; therefore, they do not have the confidence to be decisive.

GENERATE RESPECT

Instill in your children and those you influence that a fulfilling sense of self-esteem is earned and based on behaviors that reinforce their sense of self-worth and self-respect. Those behaviors should be a positive reflection and understanding of their core values. The key benefit to earning self-esteem, for young and old alike, is increased self-confidence and a greater ability to be strongly decisive when challenged with tough decisions, both personally and professionally.

19. THE GIFT OF INTUITION – TRUST IT!

You've likely had numerous occasions in life where you had to make a major decision regarding careers, relationships, residences, investments, family, children, and other realms of life responsibilities that have significantly impacted your happiness, fulfillment, and contentment. What are the primary factors that formulate a correct decision? What influences have impacted your decision making process? Did you make a decision? Or were the fears of failure and/or rejection too strong to prevent you from being decisive? Do you ever employ faith or some spiritual influence as an ingredient in a decision? Are you more analytical or emotional in making your final choice?

Chances are you've been around the block of life experience a few times, and in the process have gained valuable experience to build upon a sense of personal confidence and self-respect. Believe in that sense of self, and believe in the confidence you possess to make a correct decision. The core values that collectively form the personality of your character are the foundation for your confidence and create a subconscious intuitive ability for you to make the correct choice when the challenge of making a decision arises. I have found that my intuition, an understanding of my core values, respect for myself, and a gut felt sense of what is right have been the catalysts in propelling me to be confident, insightful, and decisive.

YOUR INNER VOICE DOESN'T LIE

Intuition is defined as "a thing that one knows or considers likely from instinctive feeling rather than conscious reasoning." Every generation has economic and social stressors, and these things increase the need for people to be more conscientious and analytical in regard to how we live on a daily basis. However, never neglect what your intuition may be telling you.

Intuition should be thoughtful not spontaneous, and intuition collectively with diligent research will equal a successful decision made. Always take the time to weigh the pros and cons of a decision, and consider all the factors involved in coming to a right conclusion. It is this combination of being analytical and intuitively thoughtful that is extremely influential in making the right decision. It is difficult to regret a choice that collectively feels so right.

Another area that influences your intuitive thought process is your degree of spirituality. I am not recommending a belief in any specific structured religion or deity; that is a personal choice. However, I am encouraging that you have a belief in something greater than yourself, and the possibility to acknowledge that you don't have all the answers, all the time. My belief in something greater than myself adds to the level of trust I have in my ability to make the right choice. I trust there is a reason for everything, and what happens to you happens for you. When life is overwhelming, it is emotionally and physically healthier to believe there is a purpose behind the madness.

TRUST YOURSELF

Individual purpose is created and driven through our service to others. Your faith in your own purpose will intuitively impact your success in making correct and core value based decisions. It has been and will be your choices that create and define who you are. Everyone has made both good and bad decisions. It is how you handle your mistakes that determines your character, and it is how you contend with success that determines your level of humility. Handle both wisely, trust your intuition, and respect yourself.

20. THE RELATIONSHIP FACTOR – "HOW'S THAT WORKIN' FOR YOU?"

For those of you who are married, have been married, or are married again, I thought I would share some insight into the relationship equation. Why are we attracted to another individual beyond the sexual or physical quotient that may result in marriage? Is it their personality, wit, self-confidence, intelligence, and/or charisma? Some people feel the other person makes them feel "complete." The truth is, though, that in any relationship the other person may compliment who you are and your character traits, but the only person who completes you is you. A solid understanding of your core values and the implementation of those values are the foundations for a complete sense of self.

In terms of whom we marry, you will discover the majority of people who marry young tend to marry an opposite. Why? Because most of these people have a subconscious belief that the other person can fill voids in any self-perceived character flaws. Where do these perceived flaws originate? Welcome into the equation…our parents.

WHY OPPOSITES ATTRACT

The primary reason many people marry an opposite is because when we were young, we were usually told everything we were NOT. "Why don't you study more? Why are you not more creative? Why can't you be more extroverted? Why don't you like the outdoors? Why aren't you more like your brother?" By the time we leave the house and venture out on our own, we have a good idea of everything we aren't.

The question is, do you embrace that knowledge and grow from it, or do you allow it to negatively impact your self-respect and self-worth? Most young adults are too immature to understand that a lack of certain parental dictated positive characteristics is not a fault of who they are as valuable human beings. They perceive, however, that if someone comes into their life who fills the voids in their self-perceived weaknesses, that person will make them whole. As a result, when they meet someone who is everything they are not, they believe this is the perfect match. "I don't study; you do. I am not creative; you are. I am introverted; you are extraverted. I hate the outdoors; you love to camp. You are just like my brother." This is a match made in heaven. Well...maybe not.

Enter another relationship "danger zone." As these individuals mature, they often become more accepting of who they are. Subsequently, everything they are may become more attractive than everything they are not. Bye-bye Mr. or Mrs. Opposite! However, the desire to be attached to someone like yourself can also have negative ramifications. You may have much in common, but if the core value base of the relationship is not in alignment, it will hinder the longevity of the relationship. Why? Who wants to be in a relationship with someone who does not reinforce the core values you believe to be important?

RESPECT YOUR RELATIONSHIPS

The key to maintaining any relationship, whether one that compliments who you are or one that fills the gaps in what you think you are not, is a unified and congruent understanding of the core values of the parties involved. Our priorities for our children, how we view the world, how we communicate our decisions, our faith, and what principles we collectively honor are a few common values that solidify a relationship.

All relationships go through trials, tribulations, and transitions, but it is and will be the synergy and strength of commitment to a couple's core values that will help them persevere through the tough times. It is my recommendation that the beginning of any new relationship begin with a discussion of those values that are important to both individuals. Core values are the framework, trust is the glue, and mutual respect is the result of a healthy relationship.

21. ALOOFNESS – MISGUIDED SELF-CONFIDENCE

Over the years, I have come to chuckle rather than be annoyed when someone with the aura of aloofness passes me by. The individual who, by their own sense of importance, looks over or down upon others is aloof. How important can someone be when he or she outwardly discards another human being? Individuals of true importance are those whose character includes selflessness and humility, not arrogance and egotism. In many cases, those who do act aloof suffer from low self-respect.

Realize that I am not referring to shyness, as it may relate to being aloof, but aloofness as it pertains to the attitude of elitism. Aloof is defined as "not friendly or forthcoming; cool and distant, conspicuously uninvolved and uninterested, typically through distaste." Have you ever asked yourself, "What did I ever do to them?" as someone walked by with that look of disdain and refused to acknowledge you? Did you appear distasteful to them? Trust me, if a person has an attitude that others are less important and less human based on outside appearance, it says more about them than the person they are disdaining.

WHAT DETERMINES IMPORTANCE?

Do the clothes we wear, cars we drive, and amount we own justify an attitude of self-importance over those who have less? I would rather enjoy the company of someone who may have less and genuinely cares for others, than someone who has more and in their mind the world revolves around them. Glitz and glamour may be fun to enjoy, participate in, read about, and observe, but when the glitz and glamour subside and the outside is no longer looking, the inside takes over.

Am I more important because I have a nicer dress or suit than someone else? Am I more important because I can eat at a fancier restaurant than those whose joy of dining out is fast food? Am I more important than a mother who can barely put food on the table, because I can afford to attend a gala? I hope those of you reading this would say, "Of course not." Yet, there are those who feel superior to others because of what they have. They fail to understand that true importance comes when you make a positive difference in the lives of others. The German philosopher Theodor Adorno stated, "He who stands aloof runs the risk of believing himself better than others and misusing his critique of society as an ideology for his private interest."

Genuine self-confidence comes from behaviors that reflect the values that form the substance of your character. Character is defined as "the mental and moral qualities distinctive to an individual," i.e. your values. Our individual values are validated by the accomplishments we have earned, not been given. If you achieve success by following the values you adhere to, and you have earned your success through hard work and diligence, how could you not be self-confident?

An appreciation for life, the things we have, and the ability to be empathetic toward others are attributes earned not provided. Each day these attributes are undermined by a growing sense of entitlement and dependency our society is progressing toward. It deteriorates an understanding of what diligence and perseverance mean in regard to generating success, and ultimately a greater sense of personal confidence and happiness. Our children are inundated by the pseudo importance of glamour and glitz rather than understanding what principles are needed to create their own uniquely successful lives.

DON'T BE FOOLED

Behind the aloofness of many is an undercurrent of insecurity and a genuine lack of self-respect. Those who sincerely respect themselves are respectful and friendly to others. Healthy self-respect negates any need to be aloof. Mark Twain stated, "A man must not hold himself aloof from the things which his friends and his community have at heart if he would be liked."

Aloofness stifles personal growth and breeds personal complacency. If I believe I am better than those around me, I have less reason to take the initiative to change and improve. Charles G. Dawes, the 30th Vice President of the United States under Calvin Coolidge, stated it best, "Mediocrity requires aloofness to preserve its dignity." Personal importance is an extension of how we generate a sense of importance in others. To be aloof is to hide behind a curtain of stuff rather than substance of character. Enjoy drawing back the curtain.

22. ENVY AND JEALOUSY –
TWINS OF EMOTIONAL DESTRUCTION

Have you ever felt a twinge of irritation or anger when someone had something and you did not? For example, a relative who married into wealth and now lives lavishly and did little to earn it, or an individual who attained a position of power only because of who they knew?

Envy is defined as "a feeling of discontented or resentful longing aroused by someone else's possessions, qualities, or luck," and jealous is defined as "feeling or showing envy of someone or their achievements and advantages." Participation in either of these two destructive behaviors is emotionally crippling and a profound waste of personal time and energy. Why would you allow someone else's possessions, title, wealth, or fame be the barometer for your own sense of dignity and value? Granted, there are many instances where life appears and is not fair, but happiness, self-worth, and self-respect are established not by what you have, but by who you are.

It is the character and core values of an individual, when implemented, that are the most memorable, meaningful, and impactful qualities of a person's legacy. I am not suggesting acceptance of unfairness in regard to human rights and human necessities, but your self-respect should not be based on a comparison between what someone else has versus what you have.

THE TRUTH ABOUT ENVY AND JEALOUSY

When you display envy, it is an indicator of your own insecurity and self-doubt. It is also a common excuse used to mitigate a lack of personal accountability in your life. It is self-defeating when you justify your own lack of achievement by comparing it to others based on envy. Envy and jealousy dismiss the necessity to take accountability for your own lack of self-perceived success by demeaning what others may have more of.

Materialism is irrelevant in regard to internal long-term happiness or the generation of respect from others. If it were relevant, then the more someone would have the happier and more respected he or she would be. Look around and you will discover materialism and long-term happiness are not necessarily congruent. There are many who have much, but do not necessarily possess the substance of character to align with it. Take away the money and possessions, and what is left is the true measure of a person's value, character, and self-respect.

If I were to be envious, I would want to be envious of another's strength of character and humility. Hopefully, those who put value on the possession of things are in balance with putting value on the responsibility and enormous importance of character. I find it distressing when fellow citizens flaunt their wealth and possessions when many others are struggling financially, looking for employment, or just attempting to make it through each day. Flaunting your possessions publically does little to unify a community or a society, but does much to divide it based on an increasing awareness of what many have versus those who do not. It is gracious and selfless to be philanthropic, but having it over publicized to revolve around the philanthropist only diminishes the genuineness of the giving.

BANISH ENVY AND JEALOUSY FOR GOOD

Here are four steps we can take to suppress the negative influences of envy and jealousy:

- Assess what it is you are actually envious of. Is it the money, the notoriety, the power, the recognition, the perceived happiness? If you had what you determine you are envious of, would that genuinely be the answer to your dissatisfaction and unhappiness? If so, what action steps are you taking to begin to achieve in that direction?

- What would bring about a sense of true personal and professional security in your life? The only way to assess that is to revisit what core values in your life are most important.

- What are you most proud of in your life? Take the time to reflect on the accomplishments and the impact you have had on others. If the effort made has been genuine, selfless, and with sincere intent, those are things to be proud of.

- If the emotions of envy or jealousy permeate, take an opportunity to redefine success in your life and determine what is most meaningful for your fulfillment.

Materialism provides comfort, but it is not the answer to long-term happiness and contentment. Remember that the things people tend to be envious about have no relevance in regard to a person's character or what someone is remembered for.

23. SARCASM –
NOT AN ALTERNATIVE TO HONEST DISCOURSE

Sarcasm is defined as "the use of irony to mock or convey contempt." Irony is defined as "the expression of one's meaning by using language that normally signifies the opposite." Contempt is defined as "the feeling that a person or a thing is beneath consideration, worthless, or deserving scorn."

Although sometimes humorous, sarcasm conveys to the person on the receiving end contempt, and the irony of the statement is a telling truth of what an individual sincerely believes about another. All of us have experienced the sting of sarcasm. On the surface, we normally dismiss it as a little humor, but it can also be extremely hurtful. Often, it is not the content of the statement but how the tone of the statement is expressed. Saying, "Nice haircut" in a sarcastic manner is much more than the words themselves express.

My intent in sharing this is to recommend that you monitor more closely the sarcasm you may express, and especially the sarcasm that our youth expresses to one another. The old saying, "If you have nothing positive to say about someone don't say it," is in need of being reinvigorated in our ever-increasing verbally sniping society. When someone expresses sarcasm, it is a mirror to the speaker's own insecurities. It's also a self-destructive way to strengthen self-respect. And really, how can any human being be happy when their apparent joy is the result of being verbally destructive toward another person?

WORDS STING

Sarcasm can be hurtful to the recipient, and it diminishes the character and the self-respect of the individual delivering the sarcasm. I have also found it interesting how sarcastic individuals seem gleeful and feel clever after they shoot their sarcastic venom. It is never clever to demean another person, for it is a self-poisoning attribute. In many respects, sarcasm has become a part of everyday existence. Comedians and talk show hosts, on many occasions, use sarcastic humor, and when they do it is arrogant and self-defeating. Sarcasm can be in jest, but many times it is used as an underhanded subtle attack on others.

Sarcasm is always at the expense of another person whether intentionally or unintentionally. What do we teach our children when we are an example of being sarcastic? It encourages a belief that sarcasm is an acceptable behavior and supports the allusion that a person who is talented in sarcasm possesses a positive attribute because it generates attention.

The pain of sarcasm is particularly destructive to developing relationships. The best example of this is the disrespect young men and women direct toward one another, specifically in the age range of junior and senior high school students. The effects of sarcasm are clearly felt by many young people and have a harmful impact on the development of both the giver and receiver's sense of self-respect. It is not "cool" to be degrading through sarcasm. Therefore, embolden your children and their friends to take the high road by being respectful and not degrading. It will pay dividends in the long-run and generate greater individual leadership and peer respect.

SPEAK WITH RESPECT

In the process of conducting constructive discourse in an adult or business setting, there is no place for sarcasm. It distracts attention away from the discourse and redirects purposeful discussion to personal accusations and innuendos. I have also witnessed sarcasm being used when one side of a discussion is losing the dialogue and their talking points become less effective and dominant. In many cases, people use sarcastic remarks as a defense mechanism to attempt to relinquish accountability for the potential negative outcome of the discourse. Inevitably, this is a losing strategy personally and professionally.

Sarcasm is an attempt to substantiate superior intellect over others and justify an elitist attitude. It may appear clever and humorous at the time it is used, but no one takes sarcasm as a serious indicator of an individual's level of intelligence, integrity, and character. It diminishes individual credibility and negatively impacts how serious a person's opinions are respected. Most important, it deteriorates the amount of trust that is established. Inherently we do not trust those who are sarcastic toward others. So enjoy taking the high road and establishing an example that is respected by those around you.

24. HUMILITY – HOW IMPORTANT ARE YOU?

How do we distinguish between someone who is confident versus egotistical? I find it fascinating how many times ego is used to denigrate others and as rationale to negate another's reputation and accomplishments. In addition, blaming someone's ego is commonly used as an excuse by blamers to lessen their own insecurities and non-accomplishments.

With that said, can you have a healthy ego? I believe so. Ego is defined as "a person's sense of self-esteem or self-importance." Through the course of our life it is essential to have a healthy sense of those traits to generate personal courage in all aspects of our decision making process. This illustrates a direct correlation between self-confidence and decisiveness.

When does being confident transition to egotism? Confidence is defined as "a feeling of self-assurance arising from one's appreciation of one's own abilities and qualities," and egotism is defined as "the practice of talking and thinking about oneself excessively because of an undue sense of self-importance." The answer in distinguishing which characteristic a person possesses lies in the motivation behind the actions being taken and/or the decisions being made by that person.

When someone's sense of self-importance takes precedence over the importance of service to others, egotism prevails. This degree of self-importance has demoralized and deteriorated the very fabric of what is the genuine key to personal fulfillment: the understanding that service to others brings with it a healthy and valuable ego and a personal fulfillment that is unselfish.

I am not suggesting you neglect yourself. I am suggesting that when you make your decisions, make sure they are not hurtful or at the expense of others. The accelerated societal obsession with personal gain (it's all about me) has corroded community values, corrupted many in power, and bankrupted our economy. If you have ever associated with a person who thinks the world revolves around him or her, then you have experienced egotism. It is the comprehension that the world does not revolve around our own agenda that creates a healthy relationship with others, both personally and professionally.

What does it mean to be important? Do you perceive yourself as being important? Your degree of genuine importance originates from how important you become to others. When your actions result in the betterment of others' lives, you have initiated being valuable.

HUMBLE IMPORTANCE

Can someone be important and possess humility? Humility is defined as "a modest or low view of one's own importance; humbleness." So how can someone have a low view of one's own importance and be important? Although it appears the two are incongruent, importance and humility can be very unifying. An individual can become very important, i.e. valuable to others, without having to self-glorify his or her accomplishments. You may realize you are important, but understanding the motive for that importance is the key to maintaining humility. Humility is not weakness in character but rather a selfless approach to very effective leadership. Although challenging to be unselfish, the rewards are far more meaningful and enduring.

In the course of my training sessions, humility is a term people rarely respond with when I ask, "What are some characteristics of effective leaders?" However, when discussed, participants gain great insight when they realize that humility by the leader provides a sense of respect and appreciation for the followers. It also demonstrates a genuine respect for individual and group efforts in their successful achievements. Humility is a silent strength of leadership respected and appreciated by those who value their leaders and how important the leader's actions and decisions may be in their lives.

Three steps you can practice to incorporate more humility in your life are:

- Think more of others than yourself

- Understand your motivation in service to others

- Give credit to those who believe in you when success is achieved

Each day brings with it the opportunity to appreciate those around us and to enjoy the many blessings we have. Set an example of respect, sincerity, genuineness, and selflessness, and your importance will be revealed to those you serve.

25. RESILIENCE – TIME TO TOUGHEN UP

Have you ever been down in the dumps, questioned your life's purpose, or failed at something and subsequently asked yourself, "Where do I go from here?" We all reach periods in our life that challenge our very being and force us to take actions that are difficult and even frightening. Choosing to take those daunting actions will forever solidify the nature of your character, your self-acceptance, and your self-respect.

The unknown crossroads we all encounter bring forth life lessons that pave the way for our future, happiness, and fulfillment. They present us with turning points or forks in the road; the ultimate decision of which path to take will contribute to what your life will become. Those actions will also formulate the answer to the question, "What will you be remembered for?"

The behavioral attribute and resource to harness the strength to be decisive and eventually persevere through uncertainty is individual resilience. Resilience is defined as "able to withstand or recover quickly from difficult conditions; able to recoil or spring back into shape after bending, stretching, or being compressed." Resilience will triumph over self-doubt, failure, and a lack of self-respect every time.

Resilience fuels perseverance, which accelerates the journey to success. A solid level of resilience rests in the core values you believe in, but most important, it is acting on and living a life reflective of those core values. Acting on your core values resiliently promotes every other characteristic of success, including integrity, personal honesty, accountability, self-respect, attitude, professionalism, humility, and empathy to name a few. A saying attributed to the Chinese Philosopher Chuang Tzu states, "Heaven is internal, humanity external, and virtue comes from the heavenly. Know heaven and humanity's actions; root yourself in heaven and follow virtue. Then you can bend, stretch, rush forward, or hold back, because you will always return to the core and it will be said you have achieved the supreme."

REWARDS OF RESILIENCY

Recognizing the interdependency of the many principles of success resulting from your resiliency will provide you with a blueprint for self-understanding and achievement. You are the architect of your life's design and the construction manager of its progress. The rewards for being resilient include learning from the struggle, adding a new life experience, reflecting with a different perspective, and gaining a greater appreciation for what you have.

The birth of resilient behavior stems from our upbringing and the parental and environmental influences we experienced. It is widely accepted that growing up around resilient individuals strengthens a person's resiliency. Most important, we all have the ability to be resilient by practicing the core values we believe in. It is bouncing back from failure and disappointment that puts the spring in our step because it provides self-confidence to carry on.

The American Psychological Association suggests that "10 Ways to Build Resilience" are:

- Maintain good relationships with close family members, friends, and others.

- Avoid seeing crises or stressful events as unbearable problems.

- Accept circumstances that cannot be changed.

- Develop realistic goals and move toward them.

- Take decisive action in adverse situations.

- Look for opportunities of self-discovery after a struggle with loss.

- Develop self-confidence.

- Keep a long-term perspective and consider the stressful events in a broader context.

- Maintain a hopeful outlook, expecting good things and visualizing what is wished.

- Take care of one's mind and body, exercising regularly, paying attention to one's own needs and feelings, and engaging in relaxing activities that one enjoys.

Additionally, believe you have the ability to be resilient and pursue the dreams you wish for. I genuinely believe everyone wants to be the best they possibly can be in all facets of life. We have all made mistake and we will make others along our life's journey, but as Friedrich Nietzsche so simply stated, "That which does not destroy, strengthens." Enjoy the strength in being you.

26. SEPARATION ANXIETY – THE PARENT GUILT TRIP

If you have ever had a child display a lack of proper judgment, or will have a child exhibit poor judgment, then keep reading. Is it possible to separate your children's successes and failures from your own sense of self-worth or self-doubt as a parent? If you are and have been a committed and loving parent, I believe this is a very difficult question to answer with "yes."

A sincere and genuinely dedicated parent takes delight and pride when their children succeed, and they frequently blame themselves and feel guilty when their children behaviorally falter. However, there is a time to accept that your children/teenagers/young adults are responsible for their own mistakes, and that those mistakes are not always a direct reflection of your parental failures. That time comes when the children know and acknowledge what positive values and appropriate behaviors are expected from them, and they choose not to act on that knowledge.

Many parents work years to instill values and ensure that their children grow up to be successful and responsible human beings. Why, then, do children who were raised by wholehearted, resolute, and capable parents sometimes make illogical and ill-judged decisions? There are hundreds of potential legitimate explanations, but if the child is making the inappropriate decision on his or her own, with full knowledge of expected appropriate behaviors taught, it is not always a reflection of the parent.

As someone who espouses core values and accountability (and who is also a parent), does a time come when I must separate my emotional attachments to my children from the lessons they must learn themselves? For example, if I put into practice the core values I champion, and I am accountable for my own behaviors, and in turn my child violates the principles I hold true, is it a reflection of me? It does not mean I do not care or am not concerned about my child, but it does mean I need to understand I am not a shameful person.

RELEASE THE GUILT

It is not necessary, appropriate, nor emotionally healthy to blame yourself when your children violate the principles you have taught and exemplified. I understand this is much easier said than done, but it is essential for your own well being as an individual and as a parent to maintain a level of emotional stability. The feeling of responsibility always remains, but hopefully not to the point where blaming yourself results in emotional and physical deterioration.

I share this to comfort the many responsible and devout parents who have gone through, or will go through, a mistake made by their own children. All parents experience the conundrum of a child's mistake, and it is devastating, sad, and so incredibly disappointing. We may beat ourselves up for hours in a malaise of frustration and disgruntlement, asking ourselves, "What did I do wrong? What am I doing to myself? What did my child do to me?" The answers are, "You did nothing wrong. You are emotionally damaging yourself. Your child did nothing directly to you."

It is your choice to allow the child's mistake to be an emotionally destructive force in the aftermath of that behavior. The child did not force you to take on that emotional burden. Of course, it does not diminish the potential seriousness of the situation, nor the responsibility as a parent to handle certain aspects related to the circumstance.

LET THEM LEARN

Any conscientious parent feels responsible for their children, but you are not responsible for the decisions your children make that violate the very values you have exemplified and attempted to instill in them. You do not hang your children out to dry, but they have to discover their own sense of personal responsibility and credibility. Hopefully, they will learn from their mistakes.

In the end, the family's core values will persevere. That strength is essential for the success of our children as future parents and their commitment to instilling core values and personal accountability in their own children. It is a challenge for all of us when we experience difficult times with our children, but it is a challenge that tests the strength of our own character, self-respect, and commitment to our own core values. Let us all be confident in knowing we can pass the test.

SECTION FOUR

BE PERSONALLY HONEST – YOUR PATH TO FULFILLMENT

"It takes courage to grow up and become who you really are."
—e.e. cummings

Nothing in your life will matter if you're not honest—honest with yourself, with who you really are, and with what you believe in. When you are true to yourself, you're more likely to be true to other people.

In life, what you value is what you think about most. What you think about most is what you become and what you attract. That's why it's important you hold dear to your heart the values you believe in and honestly display them every day.

Unfortunately, many people disguise who they really are so they can live up to someone else's expectations. In other words, they may say that they value certain things, such as being accountable or being honest, yet their actions say something very different. These people are not displaying personal honesty and they are not being true to themselves. As a result, their personal and professional success will be limited.

Remember that you can only lie for so long until those lies catch up with you. Even if you're not telling an outright verbal lie, when your actions lie about your values, consequences are sure to follow.

The principles in this section are designed to help you think and act in ways that are congruent with the core values you've identified for yourself. They're meant to enable you to "walk your talk" and proudly be true to who you are and what you stand for. My goal is that your outer self matches your inner self at all times.

Always remember that no matter what you encounter in life—whether it be a success or a setback—when you're honest with yourself and true to your values, you'll always feel a sense of self-respect and honor. Personal honesty is the bridge that will help you cross the chasms of life and reach your ultimate destination.

27. PERSONAL HONESTY – LET'S BE REAL

Through your behaviors, do you live a life demonstrating what you believe in, or do you wake up every morning just attempting to prove to the world how wonderful you are, regardless of what behaviors might be needed to accomplish that? If what you are attempting to prove is not a reflection of who you truly are, then true happiness may be elusive because you'll be in constant conflict with yourself.

Is there is a direct correlation between money, things, and genuine happiness? If the answer is yes, then it's safe to conclude that the more money and things an individual possesses, the happier and more fulfilled they would be. Correct? Why, then, are so many people who have so many things absolutely miserable? In contrast, why do some people have limited material possessions, yet they are very happy and content with their lives?

The fact is that "things" do not define who we are; rather, our "behaviors" do. If you acquire things as a substitute for being accountable for your behaviors, then you are being dishonest with yourself. Therefore, neither what you own nor the power you gain will ever fill that void in personal honesty. As a result, you may have things but be unhappy.

Material things can provide pleasure, but they are not the root to long-term contentment. I enjoy nice things, and I feel fortunate that I have been able to create a level of comfort for my family and myself. However, what I wear, what I drive, and how big a house I live in does not, by itself, define the true character of who I am as a professional, a husband, and a father. How I treat my own family, how I treat my clients, how kind and respectful I am to others, how well I conduct my business, and how accurately I practice the message I share are what ultimately defines whether I am a person of personal honesty.

DEVELOP A CLEAR SENSE OF SELF

I have made mistakes, and I am sure I'll make more mistakes in the future. But to repeat a pattern of behavior that sabotages my own sense of self and those close to me is inexcusable. Personal honesty stems from living a life that is a true reflection of who we are, and it complements what we professionally represent to those around us.

How many leaders in government, Hollywood, professional athletics, corporations, religious institutions, and many other professions disappointed and/or destroyed their family, friends, and followers with personal dishonesty? I'm sure we can all cite quite a few examples. What message do we send our children in regard to personal responsibility, accountability, integrity, and character when pundits make excuses for the personal irresponsible behavior of those in famous positions? The message sent is one that creates distrust toward others, and in the minds of many that character, integrity, accountability—the sum of which equals personal honesty—are irrelevant in regard to personal and professional achievement.

Why would any leader with significant influence and power disintegrate the very core values they are attempting to espouse to? It is called egoism, narcissism, and behaving in an egocentric manner. By definition, egoism is "the quality of thinking or acting with only oneself and one's own interests in mind; preoccupation with one's own welfare and advancement." Narcissism is defined as "excessive admiration of oneself." Egocentric is defined as "thinking or acting with the view that one's self is the center, object, and norm of all experience." These three destructive traits have historically destroyed individuals, families, careers, communities, governments, empires, and have even extended to the destruction of entire societies.

I can honestly share that my life changed when I realized the more I think of others the happier I tend to be. I also realized that it is not about me, but my service to those around me. I have learned it is so vitally important to do everything I can to ensure that the way I want the world to be, and the way I want the world to view me as being, is a true reflection of who I am. Displaying personal honesty during the course of our life is a rewarding challenge for anyone. It's a challenge I dare you to take on.

28. NEEDS AND FEARS – CATALYSTS FOR DECISION MAKING

Have you ever asked yourself, "Why did I make the choices I have made in my life? What inspired me to select a certain educational path, my profession, a location to live, a significant other?"

Two primary stimuli impacting our choices are needs and fears, which originate during our childhood. Human beings naturally direct themselves to what they perceive they need and distance themselves from what they perceive they fear. For example, if you experience an event as a child that makes you feel less valued than your friends and others in society, you may develop a need to be appreciated. Subsequently, this **need** to be appreciated will markedly influence your future decision-making process. You will make decisions in order to gain appreciation.

What if at a young age you experience the loss of someone very close to you, an event that magnified your awareness of loss, pain, and abandonment? This will result in a substantial **fear** of intimacy, because you never again want to endure those depressing and wounding emotions. This will significantly affect decisions made in regard to future relationships. You may express love for someone, but there will be a limit to how emotionally intimate you become with them, based on how vulnerable you are to the destructive emotions generated from that childhood loss.

RECOGNIZE NEEDS AND FEARS

These needs and fears create two worlds:

- One is the way you want the world to be and the way you want the world to view you as being

- The other is a world that is a true reflection of who you are

- If the way you want the world to be and the way you want the world to view you as being is not in alignment with a true reflection of who you are, you are in personal conflict with yourself.

Neglecting an awareness of your needs and fears creates an imbalance in recognizing your own personal identity. You'll make decisions to satisfy the needs and fears, which may not be in alignment with your core values and not correlate with what brings you honest fulfillment. For example, if you strive for appreciation and in the process compromise your values, you are being internally disingenuous.

To illustrate how this lack of alignment can create personal conflict, let me use myself as an example. After the passing of my father when I was eleven, I entered the seventh grade. I passed seventh grade, but my mother sensed it was an emotionally difficult year for me and had me repeat the seventh grade. To this day, I can still vividly remember walking into seventh grade, for a second year in a row, seeing many friends and teachers I knew, and I immediately perceived they all thought I was stupid—a repeater.

Hmmm…How do I make up for that apparent stupidity and attain a level of equal appreciation among my peers? By becoming a class clown, achieving in sports, running for class office, being a team captain, proving to people I am not stupid by attending West Point, majoring in nuclear physics, being an Airborne Ranger, becoming a corporate sales leader, starting my own business, being a public speaker, authoring a book? That should attain abundant appreciation, shouldn't it? And does it really matter how I got it? I'm appreciated!

However, the real question is not how many others appreciate me, but rather how much do I appreciate myself based on how I achieved that appreciation? What if I compromised what I believe in? Wait! Why should I have to answer that question? I am doing just fine. I drive a nice car, live in a nice neighborhood, and have a nice house. How could it possibly be any of my behaviors causing this internal conflict? And, if it has been my behaviors, then I have to ask myself, what do I honestly stand for and believe in, and what core values genuinely reflect who I am?

There is no way I want to have to answer that question because then I may have to reflect on some personal core values I have violated. And that won't be fun, as then I will have to hold myself accountable. Forget having to contend with that. Plus, I am doing everything everyone would have wanted me to do. I am doing just fine. Therefore, this conflict cannot be the result of me; my internal struggle must be the result of someone or everybody else. That's it! So I walk in my house, with my lovely wife and children present, and how do I behave? Am I kind, loving, a good listener? No. On the contrary, since I am in conflict with myself I behave in a manner where I may be destructive and disrespectful because I don't want to have to deal with me. A "button" is pushed, an argument ensues, the kids get involved, and now there is mayhem in the house. For me this is perfect, why? I do not have to contend with myself. I can point even to my own family and say, "See, I'm not appreciated." Now I can justify any behavior I want. I can lie, cheat, be dishonorable, because it is their fault.

GET REAL

The reality is, every time we redirect personal responsibility to others we are dishonest with ourselves. It explains perfectly why individuals can have things like title, wealth, and fame and be absolutely miserable. Therefore, take the time to validate those core values that reflect who you are, and ensure the needs and fears in your life are not distracting you from a path that is purposeful, sincere, and most important, a true reflection of you.

29. INTEGRITY – A PROFILE OF INDIVIDUAL CHARACTER

Having core values that guide your life is important. Equally important is to define for yourself and the people you influence what you mean by what you say. For example, I can say the words "love" or "discrimination," and people will define these terms based on their life experiences. In other words, a person's understanding of what love means develops through the healthy and/or unhealthy relationships that person experiences in life. Similarly, a person who has never witnessed discrimination directed toward him or her will have a different interpretation of the word than someone who has experienced discrimination.

The beauty of humanity is that we all come into this world wearing a different pair of glasses, and based on our life experiences we all see the world differently. It is that individual outlook that makes each of us unique and wonderful. It is also what allows us to learn from each other and appreciate the differences among us. Can you imagine what a world it could be if this understanding was universally appreciated and understood?

BE CONSISTENT

Integrity can be a core value, is a positive leadership trait, and is a principle of behavior used commonly to define the character of a person. But I ask you, "What is integrity?" Integrity is defined as "the quality of being honest and having strong moral principles; moral uprightness." How do you know if a person possesses integrity? Before you answer that, consider how you feel when you deal with people who are indecisive, who say one thing one day and then do something else the next day, and who are inconsistent. Chances are you don't appreciate that sort of behavior. When you are around individuals like this, you likely lose respect for them, which depreciates their credibility.

Consistency in behavior is the first step to understanding if a person has integrity. The only way I can be consistent in my behavior is to understand what I stand for and believe in—my other core values. However, I cannot leave integrity at just consistency in behavior. Many individuals are consistent in their convictions and beliefs, and in the process they have destroyed societies and decimated humanity. As referenced in the definition above, the other component that gives integrity its meaning, and therefore credibility, is morality.

What is morality? Morality is defined as "the extent to which an action is right or wrong." Certainly, that definition can be left to an enormous amount of interpretation. After all, some people believe that exterminating others who do not believe in the same God as they do is completely moral. Regardless of some form of structured religion, I define morality in my life as how I treat another human being, and I believe we should treat one another with dignity and respect.

A BLUEPRINT FOR LIVING EACH DAY

If I can wake up every day knowing what I stand for and believe in and act in congruence with those core values, and in the process treat people with dignity and respect, then I will sleep well that night and feel good about the example I set that day. As a result, I will have demonstrated integrity, resulting in a greater likelihood that I am being more personally honest with myself. This in turn allows me to hold myself and others accountable. The key to making fewer excuses is living a life that is a true reflection of who you are.

Integrity is the barometer in evaluating the level of trust within a relationship, family, and organization. Trust is the glue of every established human connection. When trust is broken, the relationship is never the same. It is comparable to a broken bone. It may heal, but it is never what it was. Therefore, keep the bond of your relationships continually strong by consistently striving to be a person of integrity. By living a life of integrity and maintaining that bond of trust with those around you, you will have established the character of an individual respected by all.

30. AUTHENTICITY – CELEBRATE BEING YOU

What does it mean to be authentic? Although I believe that we as humans have more in common than we do different, our differences create our individual authenticity. In other words, we are all unique, but it is our uniqueness in conjunction to living an honest life that creates personal authenticity.

Authentic is defined as "of undisputed origin; genuine; relating to or denoting an emotionally appropriate, significant, purposive, and responsible mode of human life." Each of us is genuine when the behaviors that reflect our personality are honest, and each of us has the opportunity to create a responsible mode of human life.

WHAT MAKES YOU AUTHENTIC?

Your talents, skills, and personality create the substance of your uniqueness, and when applied honestly you develop your authenticity. We all have the potential to be individually authentic, and it is uplifting to think of yourself as someone who is authentic based on the structure of your character and personality. Personality is defined as "the combination of characteristics that form an individual's distinctive character; qualities that make someone interesting or popular."

Being authentic is not about creating behavioral characteristics that are not truly reflective of the person you are just to please others for acceptance. Authenticity is not covering up your own weaknesses by pretending to be someone you are not. Someone who is authentic is true to his or her values and will develop a substance of character and behavior that reflects those values.

Each day external societal pressures and influences challenge our ability to maintain our authenticity. The need for advancement, the desire for money and power, the promise of immediate gratification and material abundance are all factors that have the potential to compromise our ability to maintain authenticity. When you succumb to needs that are not in alignment with your values, you are violating what it means to be authentic. Authenticity in psychology refers to the attempt to live one's life according to the needs of one's inner being, rather than the demands of society or one's early conditioning. Does your personal definition of success compliment your authenticity, or have the demands of society deterred you away from a genuine sense of self?

I believe a genuinely authentic person is never dishonest. To be disingenuous is the antithesis of being authentic. The key to embracing your authenticity is behaving in a way that reflects the trueness of who you are rather than displaying what you want others to perceive you as being. Authenticity is honesty with self, and honesty with self is acceptance of self. Taking ownership for the wonderment of you, and knowing that it is never at the expense of others, is an authentic spirit of your character and identity.

KNOW THYSELF

Outward identity comes from the adaptation of your values to your personality for the benefit of those around you. Think about what makes you wonderful and celebrate the authenticity that you possess. Your authenticity is most readily revealed in the company of family and friends. They know when you are disingenuous and violating the trueness of your character. They have been there in good times and bad and have witnessed what makes you unique. To betray family and friends is the ultimate betrayal of self.

A key to fulfillment is to acknowledge and be accountable for the times you violate your authenticity. Doing so allows you to maintain a path that is in alignment with what makes you authentic. How many people are living a life that is a true reflection of what they honestly believe about themselves? If you're not one of those people, you have little capability to be authentic.

Embrace the beauty of who you are. You have an authentic purpose in life, and you matter. The revelation in discovering your own authenticity is when your behaviors are consistent with your values, your personality is mutually respectful of others yet unique to yourself, and honesty is present in all that you do. To utilize your authenticity to enhance the lives of those around you only exemplifies the value of you and your greatness in being authentic.

31. HONOR VERSUS FRIENDSHIP – A BATTLE FOR THE AGES

Our nation is transitioning toward the biggest federal government infiltration into our lives since the New Deal. As a society, how did we ever return to this archaic juncture of dependency? I believe it has not been the result of the masses, but rather the self-centered agendas of some powerful corporate, financial, media, and political leaders. We have certainly witnessed the destructive aftermath of their wrath of greed and power.

I often wonder how unscrupulous individuals can sleep at night knowing they acquired their riches by destroying people's lives. As a society, have we lost an understanding of what it means to be honorable? Honor is defined as "personal integrity maintained without legal or other obligation; nobility of mind; probity." Let us imagine a society where all individuals and leaders maintain honor without allowing outside influence, power, and greed to compromise their ability to make a decision for the greater good—a society where we all have "nobility of mind." What an amazing world it would be!

WHAT WOULD YOU DO?

West Point has the motto "Duty, Honor, Country," with a strict honor code that states, "A cadet will not lie, cheat, steal, or tolerate those who do." This honor code is instilled in every cadet and agreed to in writing from the moment they enter.

During my sophomore year, I was dealt a personal challenge that tested friendship against adherence to the honor code. My roommate and I had the same deadline for the submission of a research paper. We were both enrolled in the same course, but we each had a different professor. Although I had finished my research, I did not initiate the writing of my paper until the night before the paper was due.

Coincidently, my roommate had not begun the writing of his paper either. The difference between us that night was that I completed the writing of my paper that evening, whereas my roommate decided to "hit the sack" without writing anything. To my surprise, the following morning we both submitted our assignments. A week had gone by before our research papers were returned to us. Upon seeing my roommate's graded paper on his desk, I noticed that his paper looked almost identical in content, sentence structure, grammar, and vocabulary to my paper. The bottom line: my roommate woke up after I had gone to bed that evening and copied my paper.

What do I do? What would you do? I did not lie, cheat, or steal, but if I do not report my roommate I am in violation of the honor code for tolerating his cheating. Do I choose my roommate or the honor code? Would a true friend put me in this position? Could I graduate with a good conscience knowing I had violated the honor code by tolerating someone else's violation? These are a few questions I conjured up and struggled with.

I confronted my roommate several times in an attempt to convince him to turn himself in, but to no avail. After pondering the questions and deciphering many internal deliberations, the final decision I made was to report the incident. As a result, there was a formal investigation, honor hearing, and the dismissal of my roommate from the Academy for violating the honor code. I made a commitment to abide by a code of honor that embodies an institution I decided to belong to. What would it say about me as a future leader, parent, or citizen if I had violated the very code that I agreed to uphold?

LIVE HONORABLY

I share this experience with you so you will entertain the idea of discussing with others and your children what it means to be honorable. I have no expectation that everyone would make the same decision I made, but I do have the expectation that everyone will ask themselves two key questions: "What does it mean to be honorable?" and "Am I living an honorable life?"

If, as a society, it becomes acceptable for people to make excuses for their dishonorable behavior and to not have a sense of accountability, there will no longer be any need to live honorably. To know thyself as a person with honor is to be known by others as a person of honor.

32. PERSONAL LOYALTY –
COMMITTING TO YOUR FUTURE

Does it seem these days a commitment to personal loyalty and values has taken a back seat to personal gratification and selfishness? What does it mean to be loyal, and have we lost an understanding of the importance of loyalty directed toward our values, family, community, institutions, and even the principles our nation was founded upon?

To be "loyal" is defined as "giving or showing firm and constant support or allegiance to a person or institution." Without loyalty within a family, workplace, and/or community, there is dysfunction, inefficiency, disharmony, and most important, a lack of trust, which ultimately ruins communication. I believe personal loyalty is dedication to upholding the values you believe in and the value based actions that structure your character. It is the act of not wavering from your commitment to living a life that is an honest reflection of who you are.

To be disloyal to yourself is to project an image to the outside world in contrast to how you genuinely feel about yourself. It is energizing and gratifying to meet someone who views you as you want to be viewed, but the important question is, how do you view yourself when that someone is no longer looking? Do you feel as good about you as they do? When you are loyal to your core values, divergence in self-reflection diminishes and a unified self is solidified. Personal loyalty strengthens character, self-respect, integrity, and aligns your actions with your mind, heart, and soul.

I also attach personal loyalty to family loyalty. Although those you love may not be you, your devotion to those who love you is as important to being loyal to the values you believe in. To show allegiance to the person you've partnered with and the children you have brought into this world, having shared with them the many joys, sorrows, and challenges of life, is Loyalty Class 101. A family is an extension of the personal characteristics of each member within it, and loyalty to those members ultimately contributes to the growth or dismantling of that family. Personally, I believe loyalty is non-existent in the character of a "deadbeat" dad or mom who provides for themselves but fails to care and provide for their children. Demonstrated disloyalty toward personal values and families has undermined and negated the critical importance of loyalty in our communities, our nation, and our way of life.

A COMMUNITY FOCUS

Non-personal loyalty is loyalty directed toward the leadership of the community we live in, business entity we work for, institution we belong to, and nation in which we pledge allegiance to. The degree that the mission, purpose, and vision of these areas of personal participation compliment our personal values will determine our level of loyalty to the leaders involved. In addition, issues, causes, and principles we are passionate about will significantly influence the amount of loyalty we commit to a specific person, group, establishment, or institution. The most important question to ask yourself is, "Do the values that structure my personal and family loyalty compliment and support my non-personal loyalty commitments?"

Healthy personal and non-personal loyalty results in the betterment of ourselves, our relationships, those we impact each day, and the world around us. It is being loyal to the goodness in ourselves that will reflect in the goodness of loyalty demonstrated to others. So don't throw away loyalty because it takes too much work to understand it or achieve it. Like self-respect, loyalty is not given but earned through your behaviors that reflect commitment to your values. As American Philosopher Josiah Royce stated, "Unless you can find some sort of loyalty, you cannot find unity and peace in your active living." Activate your life by being loyal to what you love.

33. FIRST DAY OF SCHOOL – NOT JUST FOR KIDS

Over the years, I have conducted numerous presentations for school districts around the country. Often, these presentations occur at the start of a new school year. During these times I hear teachers and staff share their mutual experiences of preparing to send their own children off to kindergarten or dropping them off at college. Having done both with two children of my own, I am empathetic to the emotion of parent/child separation, yet I also know the excitement that comes from seeing your child begin a new life experience. Their departure also puts to the test whether the values we as parents have attempted to instill in our children blossom in the challenges they are about to endeavor upon.

But this is also a time for parents to rediscover and be honest with themselves when the responsibility of raising their children is modified. The constant attention paid to the most important connection we have with another human being, our child, is now diminished, and a change in our perspective role as a parent evolves to another level of understanding. For many, our children validate our sense of self-worth and purpose and formulate a desire to work hard, achieve, and help create a life for them we believe will invigorate their potential to succeed. So celebrate your efforts as a mother or father. Your heartfelt intuition and commitment to the core values you believe in will provide you the gauge to measure your parenting success.

TAKE TIME FOR YOU

Throughout my years of developing and inspiring the lives of others, I have discovered it is consistency in behavior reflecting the values you instill in your children that sustains a foundation of self-worth and purpose. As your children grow, venture on their own, and leave you alone it is also a first day of school for you. It is a wonderful opportunity to pay attention to you and reflect on your own life and the direction it is taking. It is also a time to gauge how honest you have been with yourself. The freedom to have the time to ensure you are on a path that is reflective of what you want to be should be a treasured moment to create a better you.

An opportunity to rediscover you is at hand when the constant need to parent is partially replaced by the role of formal education. Of course, your role as a parent to evaluate formal education, participate in the process, adapt, and align it with positive family core values is essential to create a well-rounded educational experience for your children. The anxiety associated with having the children leave the nest is felt by all parents, but the anxiety felt once they are gone is more about oneself than those who left. All of a sudden, there is no longer the distraction of children when it comes to dealing with you and your own personal sense of self-worth and self-respect. Many of our own internal dysfunctions raise their ugly head. Do not shy away from them and do not allow them to discourage and depress your own sense of value. Embrace them as a challenge to be a better person, mother, father, professional, and example to those around you. Take time to spend on you and begin a transition to reinvigorate yourself and your relationships, and participate in the things you love to do.

CELEBRATE!

Regardless of whether children exist in your life, any day can be a first day of school for you. Therefore, here are five steps to celebrate your first day of school:

- Recognize it is not only a first day of school for your child, but also a day of renewal for you.

- Establish new goals to enhance your future personal and professional development.

- Get out and participate in events and hobbies that inspire joy in your life and provide a sense of well-being.

- Rekindle and refocus on relationships that have helped shape the beautiful person you are.

- Celebrate the happy milestone the first day of school brings with it by believing in your efforts as a parent and your child's efforts to become a person reflective of the values that represent the best in you and your family.

Use this time to honestly assess your life and where you want to go for the next leg of your life's journey. Then, with the tears of seeing them leave, enjoy the smiles seeing them succeed.

34. A SENSIBLE SIDE TO SPIRITUALITY

Although the choice to practice a formal structured religion is a personal one, the general thought of a force, energy, or entity greater than yourself adds another dimension to pondering our collective human existence and individual life's purpose. The phrase "life is not measured by the number of breaths we take, but by the moments that take our breath away" summarizes for me an acceptance of receiving a spiritual side to my existence.

Spirituality is defined as "of, relating to, or affecting the human spirit or soul as opposed to material or physical things." To be spiritual does not necessarily denote a belief in a particular deity, but it does promote the belief in something beyond our practical understanding and comprehension. That belief may transition into faith, but faith as it pertains to spirituality is an idea felt, not necessarily proven, nor necessarily understood.

There is a reason why each of us exists. Whether the purpose of our existence comes to a fruition of understanding is irrelevant in regard to it providing a catalyst to create a more fulfilling and rewarding life. A sense of spirituality contributes to a degree of peace, harmony, and service in our lives. Being spiritual also adds a mechanism to cope with aspects of the life experience where hurt, sorrow, tragedy, loss, and the unexpected may occur. This does not mean we utilize spirituality as a crutch for not taking responsibility for our actions or not having to handle difficult situations, but it does provide a sense of comfort that there may be circumstances beyond our individual control. Another's destructive behavior, the unexpected loss of a loved one, a natural tragedy that devastates thousands, and unexplained occurrences are part of human existence. Many experiences may be difficult to understand and hard to accept, but spirituality enables a greater ease for us to move forward from hurtful and heart breaking events.

PEACE OF MIND

Incorporating my own spiritual beliefs has aided me over the years in dealing with loss, failure, and disappointment. The passing of my father when I was 11 immediately comes to mind, and I believe his death has played a significant role in my choosing a speaking profession, the creation of my "No Excuse!" message, and the man I have become. To believe there is a reason behind our experiences, failures, and frailties assists us in looking toward the future instead of harboring on the past.

Collectively, there are many instances where human beings come together in a commonality of spirit to face and overcome great challenges that have befallen humankind. The relief brought to devastated societies is an example of not only unity in action and materials, but also a unity in spirit to help our fellow human beings in need. Allow your mind to think beyond this earthly place. To have the ability to possibly fathom beyond this realm is a marvelous attribute of the human mind and provides a dynamic of thought that is intriguing and energizing. We all have the freedom to spiritually believe what we want, regardless of what a government or ruling entity might dictate.

Being spiritual allows us to go beyond the confines of what we might be told to believe in and to pursue a path more personally honest, meaningful, and fulfilling. A human's body may be limited in movement and action, but the spiritual mind is limitless in thought and belief.

IMPROVE YOUR SPIRITUAL HEALTH

There are two key components to being spiritually healthy:

- One is a requirement that our spirituality has a positive motive and positive potential outcome for us as individuals and for those around us.

- The second is to be mindful of another's spirituality. You may disagree with another's spiritual outlook, belief, and practices, but if those elements are for goodness and the betterment of humankind, understanding and respect are essential.

I make a choice to surround myself with the positive side of spirituality, which I believe rests in how we treat and serve one another and how we persevere through the challenges of everyday living. As Confucius said, "If you don't know how to live as a person, how can you serve the spirit?"

SECTION FIVE

BE IN BALANCE – FINDING JOY IN ALL YOU DO

"We have overstretched our personal boundaries and forgotten that true happiness comes from living an authentic life fueled with a sense of purpose and balance."
–Dr. Kathleen Hall, stress management expert

To be truly successful, you need balance in all areas of your life. Your focus can't be on work all the time. Think about it... how many people do you know or have heard of who, in their search for success and riches, aren't successful or wealthy at all? They've stepped on everybody important in their life along the way. The fact is that you can have all the money in the world, but if you don't honor those who supported and assisted you along the way, you will not be truly successful or happy.

Life is much more satisfying when you enjoy it with family and friends. And the extent to which you love, honor, and respect others is based on how much you love, honor, and respect yourself. To honor someone is to value them. If you don't have those feelings toward yourself, how can you expect to have them for others?

The more you show appreciation for others, the happier you are likely to be. This applies to both home and work. Your personal growth is the key. The more you grow, the more you are likely to be appreciative as your understanding increases.

The principles in this section are designed to help you add balance in your life—to help you show appreciation to your friends and family so you don't lose touch with them as you embark on your journey. We are all stressed these days. And unfortunately, when under pressure, many people lash out at the very people who love them the most. Not only does this erode life balance, but it also hurts the relationship.

If you allow yourself to get caught up in what society dictates success to mean, you may begin to lose touch with who you really are. Don't be afraid to let the people closest to you know the real you, for when you do you'll be better able to share and grow with them.

No one ever said life balance was easy. If it were, everyone would lead a balanced life. True life balance takes concentration, confidence, self-esteem, a positive mental attitude, and self-control. It's a challenge, for sure, but it's a challenge worth taking on.

35. EARNING SUCCESS IN THE KITCHEN

Many years ago, upon returning home from a week of sharing my "No Excuse" message, Noni, my beautiful wife of many years, quickly introduced me to an unforgettable reality check. During the course of that week, I had become quite enamored with my apparent excellent speaking abilities, the response and praise from my audiences, and of course, the added ego boost of signing copies of my book for the adoring crowds. As a result, I intrinsically developed a small attitude, which revolved around the belief that I was quite "the man."

As I walked into the kitchen of my home, our dog, Adidas, hurried to greet me with that unconditional love only a dog can display. However, her instincts kicked in, as she sensed something was not quite copasetic. Her unconditional encounter with me was quite brief and she scurried away. My wife, having a somewhat different set of instincts, but still extremely effective, also sensed that something was amiss. Aware of my attitude, she understood the potential for subsequent destructive behaviors that might follow as a result of my "the man" mindset. Seeing me with my head a little bigger than the width of the door, Noni said, "Honey, remember one thing: just because you're a hero at work doesn't mean you're automatically a hero at home."

As my inflated ego exploded like the famous zeppelin Hindenburg, I was quickly brought down to earth with that powerful, candid, and quite unnerving statement.

YOU HAVE TO EARN IT

The truth is, Noni was right. Every day, each of us is out there in the working world earning it. We are earning our reputation, our income, our status in the community, our attainment of success, our sense of belonging, and our sense of self. The point is, when you walk through the front doors of your home at night, you have to earn it there also. If you want to receive the same recognition at home as you do at work, you have to earn it.

Isn't it amazing how we can be "all that and a bag of chips" for people we do not even know, and then go home and not be as considerate to the people who love us? How does that work? I have been there and done that.

I admit, there have been many times where I have been more patient, respectful, kind, considerate, professional, and empathetic to my clients than I have been to my own family. This is a destructive behavior that I have corrected and continue to remind myself of as the days, weeks, months, and years go by. The primary reason for that constant reflection is this: When I die, who or what will be the true measure of my success? I can assure you that it will not necessarily be my clients or what material possessions I leave behind. Rather, my wife, my children, my friends, those who love me, and the emotional impact I made on others will be the real measuring stick of my success.

YOUR EFFORTS YIELD RESULTS

As you may recall, one of my favorite quotes is, "You teach best in life what you want to learn the most." If you love something in life, one of your greatest joys is to share it with others. I have always had a passion for life and a deep interest in what brings success and happiness to people's lives. As I have grown in my life and my profession, I have come to realize the many successes I have had, and yet more important, the many mistakes I have made. As a result, my greatest joy is to share with others what I have learned from those mistakes and give credit to those who have supported me in the successes. My experiences have taught me that the result of any endeavor is usually equal to the efforts put in to it. Efforts dedicated to the earning of our resulting successes at work should be as important as the efforts dedicated to the earning of our successful family life at home. So have fun at work...and in the kitchen.

36. DINING FOR SUCCESS

Each day we are inundated with information about what we should be, should do, should wear, and should have in order to be successful. Our children are especially vulnerable to the power of the media and the ever-advancing speed of technology in influencing their perceptions of what defines success.

How do you define success? Is success defined as power, wealth, and fame? Or can it be defined as balance, contentment, and peace of mind? Or is it both? Are your daily actions supporting the achievement of what it means for you to be successful? Does your definition of success reinforce and compliment the personal and professional values you believe in? These are observations and questions everyone should reflect on and answer.

WORDS OF WISDOM

Over the centuries, many prominent figures have contributed to the understanding of what it means to be successful. To highlight a few...

- Ralph Waldo Emerson said, "Self-trust is the first secret to success."

- Booker T. Washington said, "I have learned that success is to be measured not so much by the position that one has reached in life as by the obstacles which he has overcome while trying to succeed."

- John D. Rockefeller, Jr. stated, "The secret to success is to do the common things uncommonly well"

- Mark Twain declared, "Let us be thankful for fools. But for them the rest of us could not succeed."

Success is defined as "the achievement of something desired, planned, or attempted." Notice that the definition provides no ethical code to what is desired, planned, or attempted, leaving the door open for much interpretation and discussion. I believe the definition of success is significantly more substantial than this generic dictionary version.

One of the best definitions of success I ever received was during a training session I conducted many years ago. A man stated that his definition of success was being "eager to go to work and eager to go back home." I thought that was a perfect definition because it exemplifies life balance in a wonderful way. To be equally energized and excited to participate in our profession and our family is a successful balance we all should strive for.

BRING THE MESSAGE HOME

So where does "Dining" for Success come into play? My homework assignment is for you to take time at the dinner table tonight to discuss as a couple or a family what success means. For those who have children, ask the young ones, "How do you define success?" Do you think a six-year-old might have a different answer than a sixteen-year-old? As a result, another door will open for parent participation to discuss the areas of success that you might feel to be important for them to understand.

If a person's idea of success is wealth, fame, power, and prestige, and if that person achieves it and believes those attributes are a true reflection of what that person wants and who that person is, then he or she is successful. On the other hand, if a person's idea of success is a happy family, an enjoyable profession, an inclusive community, and a strong faith, and if that person achieves it and believes those attributes are a true reflection of what that person wants and who that person is, isn't this person just as successful as the first? Of course! I have discovered that true success is the sum of achievement plus personal honesty. Achieving without compromising your character and core values in the process of that achievement is true success.

37. ESCAPE FROM EXCESS – THE KEY TO LIFE BALANCE

Here is a goal we all can strive to attain. When I was a child, my uncle would routinely say, "Everything in moderation." Although that phrase was, and still is, a commonly used expression, it was not until later in life that I took its meaning to heart in regard to balancing the many different facets of my life.

Do you take that expression seriously? Everyone needs to. When excess in one area of your life takes precedence, the other areas of your life suffer. Today, there is a societal interest in learning how to implement the work-life balance equation. Why? Because many people are yearning for balance thanks to three factors that have come into play.

- The speed and amount of information we as human beings are required to process every day consumes much of our thoughts, energy, and time. The velocity at which technology continues to advance will only add to this information download that we must contend with.

- The deterioration of society's understanding of what it means to be successful continues to inundate our mindsets. For example, if the media emphasis is directed toward only one aspect of life, such as money, then other areas of life suffer in regard to their perceived importance. Just reflect on how greed has consumed society in many respects and the horrific consequences that have occurred to our social and economic stability as a result.

- The inability for individuals to properly self-discipline, prioritize, and time manage their daily activities. Without some form of time management, how can you have the ability to allocate the appropriate time and energy to the aspects of your life that need to be addressed? If you do not organize and implement some form of structured approach in building balance, then chaos and disorganization reign supreme.

EXCESS EQUALS STRESS

Do you know anyone who is obsessive with a certain aspect of his or her life? How about someone who buys too much, drinks too much, exercises too much, plays video games too much, sits on the couch too much, pretends they are something they are not too much, eats too much, mows their lawn too much (oops, caught myself), works too much, and does many other things too much? While you may enjoy what you obsess on, it is imperative that you ensure the obsession does not create excess stress because you neglect other aspects of your life that require attention and responsible actions.

I sincerely believe that the need for excess, from some powerful corporate executives, politicians, and even elements of our own citizenry, creates many of the economic and societal stresses each generation witnesses. If we as a society do not take a step back and re-prioritize societal values, stress the importance of substance of character rather than the possession of things, and stop encouraging excess to substitute for our own insecurities, we are on a path of self-destruction. It is up to each of us to encourage personal responsibility for our lives, strength of character for our children, and recognition that we cannot ignore an understanding of the importance of balancing the many aspects of our lives. So what can we do?

- First, what aspects of your life are vital in order for you to feel fulfilled? Are those life priorities financial, physical, spiritual, familial, social, emotional, and/or career oriented?

- How are the aspects of your life prioritized? Are they in balance in regard to the time dedicated to succeeding at those important aspects?

- Are there aspects of your life that are suffering? If yes, then you are on the path to becoming aware that you need to take action. The most important action step is to acknowledge that you may not be in balance.

Remember that balance in life does not occur overnight. It takes consistent work. However, this simple awareness often provides the motivation to take the steps necessary to bring about greater happiness, contentment, and a wonderful realignment of the basics that bring personal fulfillment to fruition.

38. SMART PHONE SYNDROME – ARE WE LOSING OUR HUMANNESS

Is it me, or does it appear that Homo sapiens are physically regressing to the hunch backed ancestors they evolved from? Beware of Smart Phone Syndrome, for it is coming to a hand held, neck bending, posture slumping position near you. As the evolution of our species continues, there may be a day when human beings will not be able to lift their heads because of their progressive obsession with phone text messaging and emailing. I am exaggerating, of course, but there are some social consequences as a result of this obsession.

With my frequent business travels, it is becoming more and more apparent that technology is taking over genuine human interaction. Personally, I have also fallen into the trap of ignoring what is going on around me because of my apparent need to communicate immediately. Although I have witnessed this trend previously, it is accelerating exponentially.

Every month a new gadget is presented in the marketplace that is more technologically phenomenal than its ancestor, which only increases the desire and necessity to keep up with those advancements. The next generation Smart Phones and Smart Pads, the wave of new 3D movies and interactive video games, the speed and efficiency of our computers and search engines, the ever-expanding capability of the Internet, and the ability to literally wage war from an office chair are a smidgeon of examples in regard to the power of technology.

THE GOOD AND THE BAD

Yes, the evolution and improvement in technology has provided countless benefits to our lives. It is a testament to the achievement and potential of the human mind and spirit. However, the volume and speed of change today is becoming increasingly unmanageable to keep up with. Ignore it and you will become a fish out of water, have a business that is antiquated, and lapse back to a level of efficiency that is unacceptable.

In dissent, this constant necessity in our day-to-day lives to relate more to our machines than to our fellow human beings will degrade what it means to be human. Email versus face-to-face, text message versus actual conversation, virtual rather than real, and quantity versus quality of communication are just a few examples of what is becoming the norm.

With all this said, are we losing our humanness? Humanness is a derivative of the word human and is defined as "of or characteristic of people as opposed to God or animals or machines, of or characteristics of people's better qualities, such as kindness or sensitivity." I am not misguided enough to believe the cons of technology outweigh the pros. Technology has provided us the availability to be a global community and, when utilized properly, to do wonderful things for mankind.

My concern is the lessening of our ability to enjoy the challenge and wonderment of genuine human interaction. After all, it is easier to mindlessly text something potentially irrelevant than it is to observe and experience the environment around you. I consistently see a decrease in the number of young people who can effectively interact with an adult or another person for that matter. Eye contact, effective listening skills, and the ability to speak and express oneself succinctly are critical to personal and professional success. A lack of personal interactive communication with others stifles emotional development in regard to relationships and decreases the ability to have genuine empathy toward others.

STRENGTHEN YOUR EQ

One of the keys to maintaining our humanness is to consistently develop our emotional intelligence quotient, or EQ. Although there are many varying definitions for EQ, there is a universal acceptance of its importance in regard to communication with others, leadership of others, and effective management of one's own emotions. Certainly, IQ will assist in a person's acceptance to school and acquiring a job. But the value of a person's education and the fulfillment in a person's occupation will be the result of our humanness and our ability to implement our emotional intelligence quotient.

Therefore, inspire your children not only to achieve the "A" in school, but also to achieve the "A" in life by effectively learning how to communicate with peers, adults, teachers, coaches, and business people alike. As we continue to proceed down a path of technology, let us not forget to enjoy the wonderful journey of what it means to be human.

39. PERSONAL REJUVENATION –
AN ANTIDOTE FOR ANXIETY

Anxiety is defined as "a feeling of worry, nervousness, or unease, typically about an imminent event or something with an uncertain outcome." I've concluded that we are rapidly becoming an anxiety-plagued society.

People today are overwhelmed with having to keep up with the ever-changing advancements of technology and deciphering of information associated with that technology. There is growing concern by many in regard to our social and economic stability. What will the future bring in regard to societal values and the learned social norms that evolve? How will we adapt to the magnitude of technology and the enormous amount of information we must comprehend?

The positive aspect is our access to ever-changing events, societal unification, and technological advancements. The anxiety occurring is the result of the competition between the amount of information we must process and allocating the time to manage that information. This is a classic time management/ life balance predicament, with the difference being the volume of information we must contend with.

Have you ever been overwhelmed with email, text messages, voicemail, twittering, Facebook notifications, downloading, news, paperwork, etc., all while having to make rational decisions to boot? But think about this: Do you really need all this information? Have you created much of this anxiety yourself?

I believe we have. It is a choice whether to participate in this rapidly changing world. Now, I am not suggesting we negate the necessity of information and do not participate. But I am suggesting that when the speed of change becomes overwhelming, it's time to stop, take a deep breath, and reflect on the simpler things.

SIMPLICITY

Throughout my life, I have discovered that the simpler my life is, the happier I tend to be because there are fewer responsibilities to contend with. Personal rejuvenation is going back to the basics and appreciating the little things in life, igniting a sense of personal accomplishment and peaceful fulfillment. It's about recognizing that quality of life is a culmination of the quality of each day, and each day's joy is the awareness of what is ultimately most important to our own individual happiness. As such, I pay more attention to the little things and the phases of life that bring joy, reflection, hope, and new beginnings. It is those moments that recapture and invigorate personal and professional vitality.

Reflecting on the college graduations of my children, I was again reminded how each ending is an amazing beginning—how every phase reached in life, every failure, and every success is an opportunity to re-validate and re-energize the core values that have created who we are. Reflecting on my own failures and successes, I have learned that the biggest tragedies have taught me the most about who I am and have challenged an understanding of the core values that define me.

STEPS TO SIMPLICITY

Here are five primary steps we can all take to reinvigorate our lives and assist in squashing any anxiety, apathy, or malaise we may be experiencing.

- Establish time to participate in something you are passionate about. A walk to relax, a hike to challenge, a book to be learned, a painting to be creative, or a prayer to be thoughtful are just some suggestions that can help you take a break from the world.

- Look for quiet time along the success journey to reflect and re-focus on your objectives at hand. There is solace in quiet and an opportunity to listen to the inside instead of being distracted by the outside.

- "Do not bite off more than you can chew," as the saying goes. Realize that you may think you are getting more done with more on your agenda, but the stress of the multitude of tasks will be overwhelming and the quality of the tasks completed will be detrimentally affected. Anxiety equals an over abundance of tasks plus a lack of quality.

- Make a date to pull out old photos, picture albums, or home movies and smile, laugh, and reflect on some of the good old times. When was the last time you sat down with the family and reminisced?

- Reflect on the areas of your life that bring you the most joy and happiness, those little things that make you appreciate yourself and others.

No matter what happens in life, don't allow our ever-changing, rapidly evolving, technology filled world to diminish the simple and treasured joys that make life a blessing.

40. MEET THE PARENTS –
CELEBRATE YOUR DYSFUNCTIONS

Are you from a perfectly functional family? One of the interesting and sometimes fun characteristics among all human beings is that we are all uniquely dysfunctional. Maybe some of us more than others, but that is what makes us wonderful. Being aware and understanding of those dysfunctions are the keys to working through them and not using them as an excuse to justify why we do not have to be accountable for our own behaviors.

We all have our "stuff" to deal with. I have mine, and you have yours. But we regularly see two types of people every day:

- The first are those who use their stuff to justify why they are miserable, cannot perform their job, demonstrate disrespect toward others, are consistently negative, etc. In some cases, they even use their stuff to rationalize why they do not have to take care of the children they bring into this world.

- Then you have the second type of individual who recognizes their stuff as an opportunity to grow, learn, and become an emotionally stronger person.

Which one of those two am I? Which one are you? Reflect on your life for just a brief moment. It is the greatest challenges, disappointments, losses, failures, and self-doubts we experience, that when we persevere through them, teach us what we are capable of achieving. Without hardships in life, how do you have an opportunity to really assess and test what your values and character are composed of.

MEET YOUR FEARS

This whole concept reminds me of the classic movie, *Meet the Parents*. In this comedy movie and its sequels, Gaylord Focker and Jack Byrns are uniquely different, coming from backgrounds and having perspectives that are dynamically in contrast with one another. However, in the end, the Fockers' and the Byrns' dysfunctions and differences are overcome because they recognize they have common values, mutual respect, acceptance, a priority of happiness for their children, and the love between their respective children for each other.

The movie is also indicative of how our parents significantly influence our sense of self-worth. I believe that how we are parented affects our sense of self-respect and creates the two major fears that all of us possess. In other words, how we were parented influences our understanding of who and what we are.

One of the first fears generated in our lives results from the conflict between destructive criticism and corrective discipline. Destructive criticism is the disciplining of a behavior in a way that is demeaning and degrading to the child. An example of this would be abusive verbal and/or physical punishment. We have all been exposed to varying degrees of destructive criticism. If a child is exposed to consistent levels of destructive criticism for making a mistake, then the child develops a fear of making mistakes or a fear of failure. Granted, we all fear failure to a degree, but the strength of our beliefs and understanding of our own skills and core values will determine how much we let that fear of failure dictate our performance and our decision-making ability.

The second fear results from the conflict between conditional love and unconditional love. Unconditional love is just the pure giving of love to others without conditions. Conditional love is when conditions are place on the love provided. When a child is exposed to conditional love, they develop the fear of not being loved or the fear of rejection. Have you ever been around a person who cannot make a decision until everyone else says it's okay? If so, it is a reflection of their fear of being rejected if they make an incorrect decision. It shows a lack of self-respect because they don't have the strength to be personally and/or professionally decisive.

Fear of failure is fear of self, and fear of rejection is fear of others. The key to overcoming these fears is to first understand them in our lives and how they influence our ability to make decisions. They are not harmful things when we understand that they are a catalyst to force us to take ownership for our actions and substantiate an understanding of our own core values. That will provide us the internal strength to be decisive and emotionally strong when challenged with difficult situations and circumstances.

CELEBRATE THE DIFFERENCES

So let's all acknowledge and celebrate the dysfunctions—the stuff—in our lives. Nobody has his or her act perfectly together. Life's journey can be exciting and rewarding depending on how you prepare for and execute the trip. So pack the stuff you need and discard the stuff that weighs you down. Know that you are the decision maker for you own life. There may be, and have been, influences that push us in certain directions, but it is our self-respect and strength in our core values that stem the tide and allow us to continue on a course that is positive, constructive, fulfilling, and balanced.

41. REMEMBERING TO HONOR FAMILY AND FRIENDS – "CATS IN THE CRADLE"

When all is said and done, who truly defines whether you have attained a level of success and personal honesty that was a true reflection of who you are? I believe the answer comes from those who are closest to us—our family and friends. I am not suggesting you base your life solely on their assessment and feedback, but they know you in good times and bad, in joy and sorrow, love and anger, success and failure. So why, then, do so many people behave destructively toward those closest to them?

Many times when the challenges of life confront us, we go to those who love us for their comfort, understanding, and validation. The conflict arises when their response to our needs is not what we may want. Reflect on this element of finding contentment, because in the troubled times you face socially, economically, politically, and ethically, it will be your family and friends who will be there to help you persevere together as a team and family.

HUMBLED GRATITUDE

After a presentation in Washington, DC, I was returning to BWI Airport via a cab. During the brief transport to the airport, I talked with the driver and asked him where he was from. His response humbled me and sparked some personal reflection on my part. He responded, "Nigeria," and subsequently said, "I wake up every day thanking God for the blessing to come to this country, and thank Him for the opportunity and blessings to love my family, be with my family, and witness their opportunity to prosper and succeed in a land of freedom."

I thought to myself, how many of my fellow American citizens have expressed such appreciation for their country and their family? I hope many have, for we all should. Two songs that have always impacted me regarding this topic are Harry Chapin's "Cats in the Cradle" and Eric Clapton's "Tears in Heaven." The profound lyrics in Chapin's song include, *"I've long since retired, my son's moved away / I called him up just the other day / I said, 'I'd like to see you if you don't mind.' He said, "I'd love to, Dad, if I can find the time / You see my new job's a hassle and kids have the flu / But it's sure nice talking to you, Dad / It's been sure nice talking to you.' / And as I hung up the phone it occurred to me / He'd grown up just like me / My boy was just like me"* and the key phrase in "Tears in Heaven" is "*Would you know my name / If I saw you in heaven?*" The lyrics encourage me to contemplate two important things: 1) Have I created emotional distance with my own children, and 2) Would my children know my name in heaven?

CHERISH EACH MOMENT

My *"No Excuse!"* book is filled with inspiring quotes and anecdotes, and my favorite is entitled "To My Grown Up Son." It goes: "My hands were busy through the day; I didn't have much time to play the little games you asked me to; I didn't have much time for you: I'd wash your clothes, I'd sew and cook, but when you'd bring your picture book and ask me to share your fun I'd say, 'A little later, son.' I'd tuck you in all safe at night; and hear your prayers, turn out the light, then tiptoe softly to the door – I wish I'd stayed a minute more. For life is short, the years rush fast – a little boy grows up so fast. No longer is he at your side, his precious secrets to confide. The picture books are put away, there aren't any games to play – no goodnight kiss, no prayers to hear; that all belongs to yesteryear. My hands once busy now lie still; the days are long and hard to fill. I wish I might go back and do the little things you asked me to."

FOUR-LEGGED FAMILY

I've learned through my own experiences as well as from others that pets play a crucial role in the family unit, and they deserve respect too. This fact became clear to me the day our family had to say good-bye to Adidas, our beloved dog of 14 years. As the injection was being administered to her, I held her head softly, kissing her fur-coated neck. At that moment, I never realized how much I loved and would miss Adidas.

As I hugged her gently, I felt her heart stop and witnessed her head drop as the medication took effect. My tears became streams of emotion and remembrance. With my head buried in her nape, I thanked her for her spirit, love, and companionship she shared with my family and myself over the many years. During the course of her four-legged life, she had given us so much and had taken so little. No animosity, greed, self-centeredness, envy, jealousy, bitterness, anger, bigotry, ego, nor any other human deficiency did she ever demonstrate, only the selfless love a dog can share.

Companionship is defined as "one of a pair of things intended to complement or match each other." Anyone who has ever had an animal companion understands how perfect this definition is. It is a subtle emotional relationship that is unique, loving, and never broken. Although they are not children, our pets are an extension of our family and provide an element of belonging and togetherness that unifies what it means to be a family even further. As we shared the news of Adidas's death with family, my nephew shared a note, which stated, "All dogs go to heaven." I have no doubt.

Let us all extend a breath of selfless companionship and loyalty to those we love. As a grown man, I was surprised yet invigorated to feel an innocent love be revealed by the nature of an animal who loved me for just being me. It also provided me further validation of what is most important in life, for it is not what we possess, but rather whom we love that is everlasting. Give those you love an extra tight hug tonight, human and pet alike.

DO UNTO OTHERS...

Over the many years of my life, I have seen people on different staircases to success, but if they have stepped on everyone along the way, how happy can they be? They may have things, but they do not have deep-rooted meaningful relationships. Personal fulfillment in life is recognition of service to others and living a life purposeful in respect to the family and friends you share life with. Each day is an opportunity to be kind, loving, and respectful. Ensure there is time to share that kindness, love, and respect with those who love you. When that occurs, with a spirit of appreciation, it is a genuine reflection of personal honesty and the necessity for balance in all we do.

42. REFLECTIONS ON PARENTHOOD
FROM THE FATHER OF THE BRIDE

When my daughter Nicole got married, I was struck by how quickly time had passed since she was a little girl. Where did the years go, I wondered...and am I really this old? It also prompted me to reflect on that special bond between fathers and daughters (or parents and children for that matter).

How often do you take the time to treasure the times with your children and to reminisce on the many memories that have shaped your family? For all of you in the depths of parenting, treasure the moments and emotionally focus on those kindred times that pass in a blink of an eye. Two essential questions to ask yourself are: "What will my children remember me for?" and "What emotional legacy will I pass down to the people I love most?" It is never the memory of what someone had that is everlasting, but always the memory of what they were and the positive difference they made.

I can recall physically being there when my children were young, but I was emotionally in the pursuit of striving for "success" and building a career. At times, I was not thoughtfully mindful of what I was missing with my children because my agenda was more important. I am here to share with all of you, your agenda is never more important than the time you establish to influence and be a positive example for your children. We are all parentally challenged, and no one parent or family is perfect. However, do not miss the opportunity to establish genuine love and a mutually respectful bond with your children before they walk down that aisle themselves.

WHAT DO YOU REFLECT?

The following are several effective parenting characteristics that children learn to admire and respect as they mature:

- **Discipline** – Children are yearning for strength of character and structure in their lives.

- **Integrity** – No child, or adult for that matter, wants to be around those who are indecisive and inconsistent in their behavior.

- **Core Values** – Provide an established expectation of behavior and define the structural emotional foundation for the family.

- **Honesty** – This is the key to building trust, resulting in healthy communication and the ability to face challenges and persevere through adolescence, peer pressure, and the ever-occurring parent/child bickering.

- **Self-Esteem** – This is earned, not given. Parents are the catalyst to eliminate that sense of entitlement and "everyone else is doing it" mentality our children may possess.

- **Accountability** – The antidote for thinking our children our blameless is accountability. They are not angels, and it is not everyone else's fault for their misbehaviors and misgivings. Parents should not fall into the trap of making excuses for their children. It sends the message that "whatever" and other excuse-related verbiage is acceptable, which negates personal responsibility.

- **Manners** – These are the expression of respect and behavioral protocol within our relationships with others. As parents, we set the example in how we communicate, respect, tolerate, react to, and judge those around us. If we exemplify and communicate derogatory, discriminatory, and degrading behaviors, why would our children be any different?

Two final encouraged behaviors to exemplify are empathy and humility. To be understanding of others and be modest in our own importance is essential to establishing a sense of service for our children beyond themselves. In all areas of human ability, there are those more talented and those less talented, but for us to appreciate our skills and those of others is to respect the world we live in and the lives we impact.

Our children are an extension of us genetically, environmentally, socially, and emotionally. Although we do not create the ultimate end product, we certainly have the ability to love and mold the product as it is being produced. My daughter is someone who will always be an extension of me. I love her, respect her, and wish her all the joy the world has to offer as she ventures to achieve fullness of character, happiness, love, and contentment. To my fellow dads, always remember, a daughter may outgrow your lap, but she will never outgrow your heart.

43. TRUE FRIENDSHIP – STANDING THE TEST OF TIME

What is true friendship, and who are your genuine friends? You may have many acquaintances, but are they true friends? A friend is defined as "a person whom one knows and with whom one has a bond of mutual affection, typically exclusive of sexual or family relations."

As the days of our lives pass by with the joys and sorrows we experience, it is the presence of friends that enhance our experience of joy and provide compassion during time of sorrow. Each day of my life, the bonds and spirits of friendships are always present. It is reflective in my understanding of the golden rule: treat others as you would like to be treated.

WHAT IS A TRUE FRIEND?

A true friend inspires goodness, empathy, and mutual respect, which are the foundation for the establishment of friendship. It is a bond that transcends time and distance, and invigorates memories of happiness, fun, excitement, challenge, sadness, and perseverance all in one sphere of trust.

True friendship is not judgmental, but supportive in good times and bad. It is having the courage to care enough to share a concern about the other. It is honest and never deceptive nor manipulative. It is a unity of life between two human beings where the experiences of one are the experiences of the other. It is a mechanism of unparalleled support and love that never dies and is always appreciated. It is a relationship different from both marriage and the parental bond with children, because it is commonly formed during early and transitioning stages of life.

Lifelong friends share a journey in our personal growth different than our parents. It is a journey to grow with another at the same time, stage, and place in life, which is the glue that solidifies friendship. In similarity to parents, friends have watched us grow into what we are and have witnessed where we have come from. Friends share in our mistakes and successes, make fun of us and praise us, yet love us for who we are.

Although technology has enhanced the speed and our capability to communicate with one another, it has also created a world of pseudo friends. Social networking sites have provided an outlet to share our lives with those around us. But how many of our Internet acquaintances are really true friends? Would they ever put your agenda and needs before their own? Would they be there for you if you needed them? Do they really care about you, or is it just an opportunity to project themselves on to others?

Reflecting on the people I have come to know over many years, there are still those who shine above the rest in regard to friendship. A true friend you meet at the age of six will still be a true friend when you turn sixty.

CELEBRATE FRIENDSHIP

To explain why those we love enter our lives when they do should not be explained but just celebrated. Let the wonderment and mystery of lifelong friendships be the catalyst in a belief that we are never alone. They anchor us when the sea of life is unsteady, and yet encourage us to continue the journey. A friend is one who jumps aboard when others have abandoned ship. True friendship is selfless. It is a genuine gratitude to be part of another's life and share in all that can be shared. They do not focus on your faults, but always see your strengths. As Helen Keller stated, "With the death of every friend I love, a part of me has been buried, but their contribution to my being of happiness, strength, and understanding remains to sustain me in an altered world."

Seeing a gathering of family and friends at a special event, such as a wedding, reinforces how joyous life can be and how wonderful it is to share a piece of your own life with those you love most. It is a collective energy and unity that never dies and goes beyond the confines of this physical world. Genuine friendships create a treasure chest of love, respect, and richness in life that is priceless and forever memorable. As the beauty of a flower is expressed through its petals, so too is the beauty of who we are expressed through our friends.

SECTION SIX

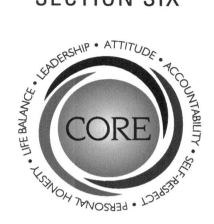

BE A PRINCIPLED LEADER – YOU ARE AN EXAMPLE

"If your actions inspire others to dream more, learn more,
do more, and become more, you are a leader."
–John Quincy Adams

You need to be the leader of your own life. You also need to allow and encourage others to do the same in their lives. We all have the capacity for leadership; whether you choose to lead is another question. Choosing to exercise your leadership capabilities by making choices is both a challenge and a joy.

Everything we've covered to this point—attitude, accountability, self-respect, personal honesty, and life balance—culminate to you becoming the principled leader you are. It's often said that leaders aren't born; they're made. That saying is so true. Your decisions dictate the outcome of your life. By you choosing to develop your core and stay true to your values, you are making yourself a leader.

The principles in this section are designed to help you become a better leader—not just of others, but also of yourself. You are not at the mercy of circumstances but rather influenced by them, and you have a proactive stake over your destiny. Also important is the fact that true leaders bring out the positive leadership qualities in others. These principles will help you develop that skill as well.

True leaders create their life based on their own expectations and not those of others. Be the leader of your life by having the courage to accept yourself and what you want to do. Adhere to core values in your heart that define who you are, and become the best leader you can possibly be.

44. PRINCIPLED LEADERSHIP – WISHFUL THINKING?

What are your expectations of a leader? What characteristics do you believe make a leader effective? Is it their honesty, charisma, knowledge, determination, communication skills, and/or fairness? Chances are, you could list a myriad of characteristics that would influence your perception of a leader's effectiveness, and any of those attributes implemented successfully may accurately define that leader.

Based on events related to the ethical downfall of high profile leaders over the years, there are times I wonder if the pure, untainted leader will be lost forever in our society. In the midst of enormous political and corporate corruption, and the increasing thirst for power, wealth, fame, and the not so almighty dollar, will there be leaders in the future who will not compromise their principles? I am hopeful there is, and I know many leaders who do maintain high ethical standards, but the trend is not promising and the negative consequences potentially significant. Most important, what are our children's expectations of those who impact and influence their lives, and how will that example affect the development of their own leadership aptitude? These are great questions to discuss around the dinner table, in the workplace, and in the classroom.

WHAT IT MEANS TO BE A LEADER

Leadership is defined as "the action of leading a group of people or an organization." How boring is that? Although a definition, it does not take into consideration the human impact of leadership and the consequences of that leadership. If the outcome is destructive in nature, is that effective leadership?

Within my training sessions, I define leadership as "the ability to lead a group of individuals to the successful accomplishment of a common purpose." However, even that definition does not take into consideration how the accomplishment was achieved. I believe the outcome of any leadership endeavor should include a component where the results were attained ethically and the outcome was beneficial to those being led, as well as the common purpose.

What does it mean to be ethical? Ethical is defined as "of or relating to moral principles or the branch of knowledge dealing with," and morality is defined as "principles concerning the distinction between right and wrong, or good and bad behavior." It is a leader's responsibility to clarify to those being led the difference between right and wrong and its relevancy to the successful achievement of the common purpose. Granted, defining right and wrong can be left to much interpretation based on the leader's ideology and even religion, but I define moral behavior as treating my fellow man and woman with dignity and respect. I am sure you would agree that now more than ever we need ethical leadership in our government, communities, businesses, schools, and homes.

RESULTS OF LEADERSHIP

In my experiences as a leader in the military, in business, in my community, and most important, in my family, I have recognized several common characteristics that are inherent in the results of effective leadership:

- A solidification of trust is generated within the entity being led, producing positive and constructive levels of communication.

- An increase in loyalty to the leader, and dedication to the mission, vision, and the core values that embody the entity we are leading.

- An increase in motivation among followers to execute the process in achieving the objective.

- The establishment of consistent professional conduct, resulting in mutual respect and dedication among those being led.

We all set an example to others on a daily basis, and the effectiveness of that example is a direct result of the approach stated above. To lead is an honored opportunity to have bestowed upon any individual, but with it comes the responsibility of leadership and the aftermath of the leader's efforts. During the process of leading those we are responsible for, it takes considerable personal strength to take accountability for the mistakes made and tremendous humility when success is achieved. Be a leader of principle, strength, and competence, but most important, be a leader of honesty and moral fortitude. There is No Excuse!

45. QUESTIONS FOR LIFE

During interactive portions of my training programs, much of the audience participation occurs because of questions I ask them directly. I am sharing several of those questions with you because of the potential impact they may have on your life when you answer them.

- **"What do you want to be remembered for?"** If you are able to respond with an answer to this question, then I hope you are living a life that is a reflection of that answer. I speak to numerous CEO groups where most of the members are responsible for many employees and millions of dollars. It is always interesting to observe the internal struggle they encounter sometimes when asked this question. The answer is so important, because if you have no idea what you want to be remembered for, then what is the purpose of the life path you are traveling? It is interesting to note that I have never remembered an individual, and the positive impact they have had on my life, based on what they owned or how much money they had. It has always been the character, values, and example the individual has demonstrated that remains the most meaningful and indelible memory of that person.

- **"Why do people follow you?"** I am not asking you to think of characteristics of leadership that you feel are important for leaders to be effective. If that was the question, you could provide a plethora of responses. What I am asking is, what leadership characteristics do you possess as an individual that inspire others to respect, admire, and look up to you? Is it your passion, fairness, empathy, attitude, determination, and/or kindness? It is extremely important to take a moment and reflect on your behavior traits that positively impact those around you. If you do not know what you do well, then how can you build upon your personal and professional strengths and attributes?

- **"How do you motivate others?"** More specifically, "How do you motivate your children, friends, colleagues, employees, and the person you are in love with?" **The best way to motivate others is to make them feel valued.** When you walk through the front doors of your place of work, do you feel like a valued employee, or just personnel? When your children come home, do they feel like valued young adults, or just kids? When you see your spouse after a week on the road, do you make him or her feel like a valued human being, or just a number? I will share with all of you if I treat my employees like personnel rather than valued people, they are less motivated to work hard and go the extra mile. If I treat my children like kids rather than valued young adults, they are less motivated to listen to their father. If I treat my wife like a number rather than a valued human being, she is less motivated to support me or my career. Without question, the workplace is more productive, a family more harmonious, and a society more humane when we all take steps to make others feel valued.

Take a moment to make those around you feel valued. This can take place with something as simple as expressing an amount of appreciation for their efforts, or sharing with them an acknowledgement of a leadership characteristic you believe they possess. I have turned around the low morale of organizations by having colleagues share with one another positive attributes about each other. As a result, those who have been on the receiving end of those comments are more dedicated and committed to the organization and their colleagues simply because they feel valued and needed.

Take a moment at the dinner table tonight and ask the children to share a positive attribute about their sibling(s). I will guarantee you those siblings will be more committed to and bonded with one another after that interaction.

Enjoy the pleasure of motivating and encouraging those around you. It is forever appreciated.

46. SUSTAINING SELF-DISCIPLINE – THE BACKBONE OF ACHIEVEMENT

During the course of my travels and speaking engagements, people frequently ask me, "What elements of your character were developed while attending West Point?" Two that come to mind consistently are *performance under pressure* and *self-discipline*, and both principles are interdependent of one another.

Having to perform under pressure ignites the practice of self-discipline. I believe societal changes, including the pampering of our children and the relinquishing of holding individuals accountable, have played havoc in understanding the importance of self-discipline.

GET TOUGH ON YOURSELF

Self-discipline is defined as "the ability to control one's feelings and overcome one's weaknesses; the ability to pursue what one thinks is right despite temptations to abandon it." Have you ever abandoned a task or dream because of the overwhelming feeling of stress, self-doubt, or awareness that an alternative course might be easier but less rewarding? Self-discipline mitigates those feelings, weaknesses, and temptations.

Increases in alcohol and drug abuse, acting upon temptations for personal gratification, and the willingness to violate one's personal core values for self-serving financial gains are all results of a loss of individual self-discipline in our society. The ever-increasing advancements in media and internet technology only fuel the fire by offering distractions that lure people away from their primary focus, a proper life path, and a difficult task at hand. A lack of self-discipline tends to always align with taking the "easy way out" or caving to temptations of personal gratification.

For example, is it easier to work on a research paper, or to play on social networking sites? Is it easier to sit down and watch the "boob tube" (literally), or work on developing your mind through constructive reading and intellectual engagement with others? Is it easier to eat cake, or say "no" and eat healthy to maintain a proper weight? Is it easier to sit on the couch and vegetate, or to exercise to improve your health and fitness? Is it easier to be ill learned, or to develop professionalism and pursue further education? Is it easier to be ill mannered and use profanity, or to utilize proper etiquette and speak succinctly? A lack of self-discipline is a primary factor for the hindrance of personal growth and professional development.

STRENGTHEN YOUR SELF-DISCIPLINE

Five steps to strengthen your self-discipline are:

- Reinforce an understanding of the core values that you believe in and reflect who you are. Define those values and incorporate them in the process of accomplishing the task at hand.

- Take "baby steps" when beginning the pursuit of a new endeavor. It is imperative not to look at the entire vision at hand, but to approach the task day-by-day.

- Establish a moral compass that is in alignment with the core values you espouse to. A clear sense of your morality will subdue the temptations of the deadly sins we are exposed to every day. Remember, I define morality as how I treat another human being, and I believe we should treat one another with dignity and respect. Take the time to assess how you would want to be treated if you were walking in another's shoes.

- Manage your time and effort by planning properly and executing the task efficiently. Prioritize the elements of the task to best reach that goal in the most efficient manner possible.

- Visualize the light at the end of the tunnel and anticipate the satisfaction of the successful completion of that goal. Concerted Effort + Determination = Self-Discipline.

There is nothing more satisfying and self-respect developing than the knowledge that your efforts and determination were the primary factors in the achievement of your success. Successful leaders are always self-disciplined in the pursuit of their passions, dreams, and goals. Be that leader and set a positive, self-disciplined example every day for those around you.

47. SIMMER DOWN – A KEY TO PROFESSIONALISM

One of the first tests in determining a level of your own personal emotional security is your proficiency in handling stressful and pressure packed situations. To create a successful communicative working atmosphere and a harmonious home environment, you need to maintain a level of emotional self-control when challenged with difficult decisions, tasks, and personnel interactions.

What is the danger of "losing it" in the workplace and at home? The primary consequence is a serious deterioration in communication between all individuals involved in an emotional meltdown taking place. If I am part of an organization where leaders and colleagues become emotional volcanoes when faced with stress and difficult decisions, constructive communication immediately declines.

The behavioral culprit that spurs this decline is typically verbal abuse and is a key indicator in evaluating your ability or inability to handle situations in a mature and professional manner. Think about it...how can a person think clearly and respond rationally when he or she is being verbally attacked? The person can't, and as a result, any chance of proactive communication is gone. In addition, the desire to avoid further communication with the attacking individual is initiated, because no one wants to be on the receiving end of verbal abuse.

Whether this occurs at work or at home, a consistent series of events takes place: Subsequent to the verbal abuse being initiated, communication deteriorates and the flow of information breaks down. If the flow of information breaks down, how could any organization be efficient, productive, and profitable? They can't. On the home front, why would a child want to listen to a parent if that parent has the tendency of belittling and verbally humiliating the child? They will not. As a result, the child avoids and turns off any desire to listen, and typically responds with the same tone and degrading verbiage as the parent. Thus, the child learns to handle stress and conflict in the same manner as the parent, resulting in a new future verbally abusive parent.

SHOW YOUR INNER STRENGTH

Former Saturday Night Live star Cheri Oteri would humorously say in one of her skits, "Simmer Down." Performance under pressure is the key to determining your inner strength, confidence, and emotional stability. I define "performance under pressure" as "an indication of one's professionalism," and I define professionalism as "emotional patience." It is paramount that your behavior reflects a high degree of professionalism when dealing with conflict, stress, and pressure. The key is being patient with your emotions and how you react to them. This emotional patience stems from your security with your personal core values, which provide the inner strength to be proficient at handling difficult situations.

For example, if I squeeze a tomato, what comes out? Grapefruit juice? Apple juice? Orange juice? Of course not! Tomato juice comes out. The same is true with human beings. When a person is squeezed (i.e. put under stress and pressure), what's inside comes out. So if an individual is internally frustrated, resentful, discontent, and jealous, to name a few destructive characteristics, I doubt seriously that the individual would display a kind, loving, and compassionate demeanor when put under emotional pressure.

Patience is still a virtue, and emotional reactivity to any situation is the barometer in evaluating your success with that virtue. Personal core values provide the building blocks to solidify a foundation of strength against life's pressures and stresses, and to maintain a high level of professionalism that demonstrates superior leadership. Have fun, be that positive example, and enjoy the stress relieving benefits of simmering down.

48. THE SALES PROFESSIONAL IN ALL OF US

After doing many presentations for sales organizations over the years, I've concluded that we are all in the profession of selling. Attributes of a successful sales professional include:

- Knowledge of the product

- Effective organizational and communication skills

- Competency in time and stress management

- An ability to mediate dissension and objections

- A high degree of confidence, professionalism, positive attitude

- The ability to provide consistent follow up and exceptional customer service.

Although you may not literally sell a product or service, in actuality you sell yourself every day to those around you and those you love. You are the product. As such, having self-respect is key.

How successful are you at selling you? Are you traveling a path of selling success to achieve your goals and surpass your quota for the year? What are the features and benefits you provide to your customers? What added value do you bring to the people and family members you associate with? Are you knowledgeable about the elements that create the product "you"?

DEVELOP YOUR PERSONAL SALES ACUMEN

Welcome to Selfless Selling 101! Following are a few skills to set you on a path to selling success.

- **How organized are you?** With the ever-increasing speed of technology and pace of life, staying organized has become increasingly stressful. However, a lack of organization combined with the onslaught of information and speed of living only increases stress and frustration. To better organize your life, pace yourself and slice each task into pieces like a pie, and don't attempt to devour the entire dessert. Something as simple as cleaning part of the garage, eliminating some stuff you do not need, or updating one piece of paperwork (i.e. a will) are a sampling of slices. The key is to take an efficient and thoughtful piece each time to ensure the results of your activities are of quality, not just quantity, enabling better preparation for tomorrow.

- **How are you marketing the product of "you" to your customers?** Your ability to communicate effectively is the basis for others to understand who you are, providing an honest representation of what they are buying.

- **Are you a good listener?** In any selling situation, listening is essential and yet it is one of the least taught communication skills. If you do not listen, how can you genuinely know what your client needs? In other words, if you do not listen more carefully to the needs of your friends and family, how can you effectively ascertain a solution to their concerns and issues. Let us all make a greater effort in making sure we listen, think before we speak, and analyze more effectively than emotionalize.

- **Do you respect your time?** With disorganization comes its best friend, improper time management, resulting in tremendous stress and emotional turmoil. Are you keeping appointments with yourself? Are you managing and scheduling your activities constructively? Do you have an appointment book, a planner, a journal, a pattern of behavior and action steps to maintain efficiency and productivity? Proper personal planning does prevent poor personal performance. Take the time to plan your day and strive for a level of consistency to maintain order in your life.

- **Are you respecting yourself?** Selling, as living life, is stressful. What are you doing to alleviate that pressure? Are you eating right, exercising, and taking time to participate in undertakings you enjoy? You can only be as effective for others as you take the time to be effective for yourself. Not taking care of your emotional and physical well-being cannot be used as an excuse to be miserable and ineffective. It is a personal choice to neglect yourself. Any accountable and competent sales professional will tell you selling can be exhausting and draining, and life is no different. To not maintain your health, energy, and stamina through the course of selling, or life, only makes the task at hand more difficult. Personal maintenance allows you to better handle crises, dissention, and provides you the courage to handle rejection and objections.

Understanding and practicing the core values that create the product of "you" provides the confidence and the ability to be professional and positive. It also enables you to provide the kind of service that every customer would want and expect. When you close each sale with sincerity, class, and humility there is no doubt you will be awarded sales professional of the year.

49. MANNERS – A REMINDER FOR YOUNG AND OLD LEADERS ALIKE

What does it mean to be mannerly? Manners are defined as "polite or well-bred social behavior," and polite is defined as "having or showing behavior that is respectful and considerate of other people."

As a society, have we lost an understanding of the significance in being mannerly toward one another? Are we too self-centered or self-absorbed with our own agendas that we carelessly disregard our behavior toward others? What mannerly path are our youth on, and what is the exemplifying trend that we as parents and adults display to our young? There is a pervasive thought that we may have lost the societal battle in creating a citizenry that is mutually respectful and considerate. I believe the battle is not lost, and it is time for all of us to initiate a resurgence in reinforcing the manners that we expect from our children and one another.

While in my local mall, I witnessed a young boy being disciplined by his mother. During the discourse, the boy turned away from his mother, lifted his arm, directed it toward her with his palm open, and stated, "Talk to the hand." Upon hearing the exchange, I reacted like the TV character Kramer walking through the door into Seinfeld's apartment, with that bodily twitching motion and stunned surprise. Subsequently, to my chagrin, the mother dismissed the behavior as being the norm and not worth committing any effort to correcting. I will say that if either of my children had ever told me to "talk to the hand" they would have been escorted out of the mall by me, taken home, and disciplined, resulting in a considerable loss of privileges.

PRACTICE MEANINGFUL ACTS OF KINDNESS

The common courtesies of "thank you," "please," and "you're welcome" should never be neglected. Small acts of kindness, such as opening a door for someone or the chivalrous behaviors men used to do for women, should not be forgotten. You may think that manners are old fashioned, out of date, and not necessary, but how is treating people with respect and kindness no longer necessary? The fact is that being polite and displaying manners are the right things to do. Whether someone responds to the courtesy is irrelevant and should not deter you from continuing to set the appropriate leadership example.

Additionally, there have been many instances where I have refused to turn a blind eye to disrespect, and I have made both young people and adults aware that their disrespect and lack of manners are not acceptable. Whether my corrective behavior is adhered to or not is again irrelevant. At least others will know where I stand and what is expected in regard to being mannerly.

Manners also pertain to a very important aspect in initiating a relationship with others, both personally and professionally. The old cliché that an individual only has one chance to make a good first impression is as important and truthful today as it ever was. That first impression is key in establishing a positive rapport with others. For example, an initial interview for potential employment, and the acquiring of that employment, will be significantly influenced by the manners the interviewee displays. In addition, how someone communicates reflects whether he or she has manners. Answering "yes" instead of "yeah," articulating your thoughts without every other word being "ah," "like," "um," "you know," etc., has a huge impact in how others perceive you. Over my many years of speaking and communicating with others, I've learned firsthand that a person's ability to communicate provides a clear illustration of the impact manners, courtesy, and respectful communication have on the other party's impression of you.

Let us all take the time to be more cognizant of how mannerly, or not mannerly, we are to one another. Let's also recognize the example we set for our children. Our little darlings are not always so darling, and educating them in understanding the important role of manners, and holding them accountable, should not be diminished by societal acceptance of behaviors that are disrespectful toward others.

50. IF YOU WERE TO DIE TOMORROW –
A LESSON IN LEADERSHIP

Some time ago, I attended a funeral for a high school classmate of mine who succumbed to her courageous five-year battle with cancer. The church was filled to capacity as the mourners reflected on her young life. The service concluded with a eulogy by her husband and father of their two children. I listened intently and compassionately to the words as he reflected on the person, wife, and mother she was. As he shared the many characteristics of a beautiful human being, I was glad to have known her. His words also triggered a further understanding of the expansive breath of what it means to be a leader. Leadership comes in all human shapes and sizes, as do moms and dads. Yet there are common threads that create the very fabric of effective leadership.

Although title, power, fame, and wealth may indicate a person in a position of leadership, that alone does not give credence to being an effective leader. This is illustrated every day in the failures and incompetence of many in positions of power as they fail to understand that genuine leadership is more about the responsibilities to others rather than themselves.

ARE YOU A LEADER?

Any person who impacts another is a leader. There are many who believe in you, count on you, and love you. If you were to die tomorrow, what would those you love and those you impacted say about you? Would you even know what you would want them to say? Are you aware of the positive leadership characteristics that are most reflective of you? These are significant questions to ponder since they relate to personal accountability and taking ownership for the path and direction your life is traveling. In other words, taking ownership for what you want to be remembered for is the key to living a life that is an honest reflection of who you are.

This task of living honorably is undermined consistently by the continued social trend toward excuse making and blaming rather than taking personal responsibility for one's own actions. Where do we find direction in how to lead effectively when those who are titled as leaders violate the very foundation of effective leadership?

Regardless of political or corporate affiliation, it is abhorrent to witness the true lack of citizen concern and irrational decision making by so many who are in positions responsible for the future direction of our society. I would enjoy some day witnessing the words "special interest" not being associated with the meaning of public service. Of course, that will never happen. I believe this route of economic irresponsibility, decline in moral objectivity, and the rupture of core-valued leadership is the result of a lack of personal ownership to the values that are most important to adhere to.

LIVE BY YOUR CONVICTIONS

What are the principles that form your decision-making and interaction with others? What are the values that define what you stand for and believe in, and are those values projected in your actions? As a minor public servant, I have always known you cannot please everyone, but I do believe you can generate respect and set a positive example by being consistent in your beliefs, remaining open-minded to others' beliefs, and treating others as you want to be treated—that being with dignity and respect.

Through the years, I have experienced a consistent number of character traits that universally translate to being an effective leader, whether it be in the office, at home, or on the battlefield. Discipline, integrity, commitment, loyalty, perseverance, honor, respect, and humility are just some that come to mind. The most important is selflessness.

Always remember that the result of your actions should always be beneficial and inspirational to others. Returning to the eulogy, it was never mentioned what she had taken during the course of her life, but rather what she had given, and therefore what she will be remembered for. Are those you love and lead better people and leaders themselves for having followed you? When the mirror reflects what you see, is that truly who you are?

51. AUTUMN – YOUR TRUE COLORS IN THE MIDST OF CHANGE

Autumn is my favorite season. Fall's distinguishing beauty of majestic colors inspires reflection and reconciliation in many. Autumn signifies that a year of hibernation, rebirth, and celebration has passed into another cycle of letting go of the past, taking ownership for our successes and failures, and establishing new and improved priorities for our future. Each leaf that turns color and falls gracefully to the ground is a metaphor for the unique change that is capable in all of us.

We each have the opportunity to display our own vibrant colors through living a life reflective of our honest character and the values we hold dear. With autumn brings a chill in the air, and an understanding that preparations must be made to persevere through a season less bright and less warm. This need to prepare for change is not only initiated by the onset of each distinctive season, but is a lesson reflective in the understanding that change is a part of our daily lives.

To ignore change and not embrace, learn, and grow from it will have the same consequences as not preparing for a frigid winter or a sweltering summer. Change potentially creates discomfort, and discomfort creates personal challenges. We all know, and have felt, what leaving our "comfort zone" is like. It forces us to adapt or stand firm, be more creative and/or innovative in our approach toward a personal or professional task.

OVERCOME THE STRESSORS OF CHANGE

The onset of change transcends into the real challenge of revisiting the core values that strengthen your ability to make the decisions to effectively confront the change. Solidifying, updating, and redefining the core values of the individual or the organization are the initial steps in building a staircase to overcome the stressors of change. As the spring and summer brought with it a new beginning and growth, each year offers the same opportunity for us as human beings. Autumn's exquisite and colorful display is a celebration of that growth. However, it also provides an understanding that we cannot eternally hold on to what was;

rather, we need to embrace another year of what could be. As each leaf falls, believing a new leaf will return in the spring stronger and healthier is the inspiration to carry on.

Consistency is comfortable, although it breeds mediocrity. An organization or individual that does not tackle the challenge of change will ultimately be defeated by the competition or life. Letting go of unwanted behaviors and destructive patterns of performance is also a wonderful benefit to dealing with change. It forces the necessity to revisit how we do things, both in a personal and professional setting. It allows us to potentially create a more efficient and productive workplace, and it sets us on a new path of personal growth and discovery.

The onset of change also tests how strong the element of trust is in any environment. Trust is the key element in one's desire to feel free to communicate, and change forces communication. Therefore, change can be a barometer for the degree of trust an organization or family has by the willingness of those involved with the change to communicate.

CHANGE IGNITES OPPORTUNITY

From a leadership perspective, change also provides an opportunity to observe another's true colors. It allows a greater awareness of how those we lead deal with the stress of change, and who has the character to embrace the opportunity rather than whine about the challenge. Change allows me to know who my future performers and leaders are, and it enables me to evaluate who may lack the determination and strength of character to handle difficult situations and decisions.

A final benefit of change is that it presents an opportunity to develop new skills, hone old ones, and expand your horizon in regard to the greater potential of what you can be. It is satisfying to display the uniqueness of your present colors, but even more to know you have the ability to create a pattern of new colors in the future. As you reflect on the magnitude of nature's canvas, celebrate knowing that a new canvas will present itself with the opportunity to paint a more vibrant, substantial, and better you.

52. AN ETHICAL RESOLUTION FOR YOUR LIFE

As you reflect on your life to date and look forward to the future, I would like to propose a slightly different goal for you—one that focuses on improving how you ethically behave and demonstrate respect toward others, resulting in countering a social trend toward unethical normalcy. I believe we are teetering on a precipice of significant moral challenge. It appears there is continued movement toward an acceptance that behaviors such as cheating, lying, philandering, etc. are more the norm rather than the exception.

As individuals, we should be resolute in enhancing an ethical example to those around us, especially our youth. With the increasing ethical landslides of so many prominent individuals, our children are undoubtedly more suspicious in believing the importance of what any leader may say. Too many leaders today behave in contrast to what they say and project to the world. Hypocrisy is defined as "the practice of claiming to have moral standards or beliefs to which one's own behavior does not conform; pretense," and ethics is defined as "moral principles that govern a person's or group's behavior." The continued corruption in so many of the most prestigious offices of business and government only fuels the social distrust machine. The hypocrisy of individuals, thereby deteriorating integrity and personal honesty, is a cycle that must be challenged.

INSTILL LEADERSHIP IN OTHERS

The necessity to live a life that is a reflection of the values we as individuals believe in is paramount in avoiding a personal moral meltdown. I would ask any parent reading this to make it a priority to revisit and reinforce with their children the internal character benefit that comes from behaving in an ethically responsible way. This will help them create a synergy between who they are and what they project to others they are, resulting in a wholesome sense of self. Our personal and family core values are the foundation for the establishment of such expectations of moral behavior. The examples we as adults set are not only critical to substantiating the expectation of moral behavior for our children, but they also have an overall societal benefit by "raising the bar" in regard to appropriate and inappropriate behavior.

Upon returning from speaking engagements, I always reflect on how many of my attendees, and therefore citizens, are yearning for moral, ethical leadership and role models. True leadership is not self-centered but selfless. With leadership comes added responsibility, and part of that responsibility is to be an ethical example to those being led. What kind of message is sent to all citizens when leaders from any arena are found to have violated the very trust they created between themselves and their followers? The message is one of disappointment and distrust.

Is there still ethical leadership? I believe there is, and many of our fellow citizens espouse to a higher calling every day. We all make mistakes—I certainly have—but our challenge should be a continuous improvement on making conscious principled choices initially, to avoid the consequences of being unethical. We have a responsibility to future generations to help create a more ethical society, for the opposite will only generate more distrust and less kindness in our world.

KEYS TO ETHICAL LEADERSHIP

Five recommendations for enhancing an ethical example are:

- Take ownership for what you say and do each day.

- Reflect to ensure your behaviors are in alignment with the values you hold dear.

- Act on the Golden Rule of treating others as you would want to be treated.

- Be consistent in what you stand for and believe in because that generates integrity.

- Realize you have a responsibility to others, for there are many who respect and believe in you and want strength of character in their lives.

It has been an honor to share with all of you some thoughts to ponder. I wish everyone the best in life. May you become the leader you know you are capable of becoming.

CONCLUSION

Knowing and living by your core values can and will dramatically improve your life. Why? Because you're the one who is primarily responsible for your future. Your future happiness and fulfillment depends upon you living a life that is a true reflection of what you believe in and having the courage to stand by your beliefs no matter what.

So I ask you, are you taking the time in the throes of chaos, life, and technology to reflect on those areas that challenge your ability to live the values you believe in? Or are you just drifting through life aimlessly, putting out fires as they arise, and hoping for the best? The more you know what you want and live a life of reflection, the better your outcomes will be.

As you delve deeper into your core values, please remember that this is a process and that change won't occur overnight. You have to take action. And even with concerted effort, substantial changes take time. But the time and effort are worth it. After all, you're going to be living in your future whether you like it or not—you might as well make it a future worth living.

As you go forth, I urge you to embrace the guiding core values of Attitude, Accountability, Self-Respect, Personal Honesty, Life Balance, and Principled Leadership. Follow that little voice in your heart and the vision in your head so you can become the best you can possibly be. Staying true to your core values is the best way to overcoming obstacles, achieving, and earning the success you deserve.

ABOUT THE AUTHOR

Internationally renowned speaker, trainer, and consultant Jay Rifenbary educates and motivates corporate teams and conference attendees through his world-class, on-site professional training and development seminars, workshops, and keynote speeches.

A resident of Saratoga Springs, NY, Jay is president of the Rifenbary Training & Development and author of the international best-seller, *No Excuse! – Incorporating Core Values, Accountability and Balance into Your Life and Career,* awarded "Book of the Year" by the North American Book Dealers Exchange.

He has provided his expertise in the areas of personal and professional core value development, leadership, and communication training to organizations, associations, and schools across North America, Europe, and Asia.

Jay received his Bachelor of Science degree from the United States Military Academy at West Point, with a concentration in Nuclear Physics.

From being a qualified Airborne/Ranger, Military Commander, Sales Professional, Corporate Manager, and Entrepreneur, Jay brings a unique background of interpersonal skills and business experience to each of his training and speaking engagements.

Within his community, Jay is and has been involved with numerous public service activities including a member of the Saratoga Springs City School District Board of Education, Board of Directors for Patriot Hills of New York, President of the Board for the Friends of the NYS Military Museum, a member of the 20th Congressional District Service Academy Selection Committee, and a columnist for the Saratogian newspaper.

He and his wife, Noni, have two adult children, Nicole and Jared.

HAVE JAY RIFENBARY SPEAK AT YOUR NEXT EVENT

Jay Rifenbary's exciting, effective approach to motivation and leadership will provide the catalyst to higher levels of achievement and productivity for your company or organization.

Ideal for corporate, education, medical, association, sales, public service, and other enterprising industries, these one-of-a-kind programs will equip your employees with the tools they need to succeed.

- No Excuse! - Incorporating Core Values, Accountability and Balance into Your Life & Career
- No Excuse! - An Action Plan for Productive and Profitable Success
- No Excuse! - An Inspirational Approach to Enhancing Educational Accountability
- No Excuse! - An Accountable Approach to Unified Care and Patient Satisfaction
- No Excuse! - Building Industry Esprit and Team Unity
- No Excuse! - Igniting Sales Performance & Professionalism
- No Excuse! - An Ethical Approach Toward Public Service

Custom programs are also available to meet your company's unique, immediate needs. For more information, contact us at:

RIFENBARY TRAINING & DEVELOPMENT
12 Bog Meadow Run • Saratoga Springs, NY 12866
p. (518) 587-6411
WWW.RIFENBARY.COM